Reality Check

Other *For Better or For Worse*® Collections

Retrospectives

Little Books

With Andie Parton

Reality Check

A *For Better or For Worse*® Collection
by Lynn Johnston

**Andrews McMeel
Publishing**

Kansas City

04 05 06 07 BBG 10 9 8 7 6 5 4 3

ISBN: 0-7407-3810-0

Library of Congress Control Number: 2003106542

Mark Cohen photo courtesy of The Ohio State University Cartoon Research Library

For my dear friend
Mark Cohen

His reality check was when he discovered he had cancer—his call to me began with, "Guess what? I'll never have to worry again about buying something with a lifetime guarantee!"

He fought against an ever-debilitating condition with a sense of humor that made us laugh through our tears. He was a cartoonist and a collector of comic art, and he represented many of us as an agent. He was honest and fair and respected by everyone who knew and worked with him.

Often, when I call his wife, Rosie, his voice still answers on the message machine: "Mark Cohen speaking! If I'd known you were going to call, I would have been here!"

Some people will always be here, Mark . . . *thanks for everything!*

Lynn

WHERE THERE'S A BILL... THERE'S A WAY!

BUY, BUY, BUY, BUY BUY, BUY, BUY.....

WRAP, WRAP, WRAP WRAP, WRAP WRAP WRAP

SEND, SEND, SEND SEND, SEND SEND....

EVERY YEAR I WONDER IF THE JOY OF GIVING EQUALS THE JOY OF GETTING THE GIVING OVER WITH!

JOHN, WHO ARE THE PHLEGMANS?

I MET THEM AT A CONVENTION, ONCE.

WHAT ABOUT ALF AN' VELDA SNELGROOT?

HAVEN'T GOT A CLUE!

AND, THE BUNG-WILLETTS?

UM.... I THINK WE'RE RELATED.

MOM, HOW COME YOU KEEP SENDING CHRISTMAS CARDS TO PEOPLE WE DON'T EVEN KNOW?

BECAUSE, THEY KEEP SENDING CARDS TO **US**!!!

RATS. THERE'S 6 MORE PEOPLE I NEVER SENT CARDS TO.

WRITE, WRITE, WRITE, WRITE, WRITE, WRITE, WRITE...

THIS PILE GOES TO CANADA. THIS PILE IS "UNITED STATES". THIS PILE IS "INTERNATIONAL".

....AND THIS PILE, I'M CALLING "QUITS"

THE TREE IS LOVELY, ELLY. YOU FOUND A NEARLY PERFECT ONE!

IT'S ARTIFICIAL DAD.

THE HOLLY LOOKS FRESH. DID IT COME FROM THE WEST COAST?

IT'S PLASTIC. I GOT IT AT "SAVE-A-BUCK".

AND THE POIN-SETTIAS?

THEY'RE SILK! THEY LOOK REAL, DON'T THEY.

SO, MAYBE I'LL TAKE THE DOGS FOR A WALK.

IN THIS WEATHER?

WHAT...YOU MEAN THAT'S **NOT** "STYROFOAM"?!!

LYNN

WHAT ARE YOU SMILING ABOUT?

I'M JUST WATCHING APRIL.

JUST A FEW DAYS AGO, SHE LOOKED LIKE A MATURE YOUNG WOMAN. THERE SHE WAS, ON-STAGE IN A FORMAL GOWN PLAYING THE GUITAR.... AND NOW, LOOK AT HER.

....BUILDING A SNOW-MAN, LIKE A KID! —IT'S NICE TO KNOW SHE'S STILL "OUR LITTLE GIRL".

YOU GAVE HIM A COOL 6-PACK, APRIL!

YEAH, BUT HOW DO YOU BUILD SHOULDERS ON A STICK?

LYNN

WHAT HAPPENED, APRIL?

DAD STARTED SINGING "I'M DREAMING OF A WIDE CHRISTMAS"

HOO! THAT DUDE'S GOT A WHOLE BUSLOAD OF UNIVERSITY KIDS HEADIN' HOME FOR CHRISTMAS... HOPE HE CAN STAND THE NOISE!

LIZARDBREATH!

HEY, UGLY BROTHER!

NEED A RIDE, CANDACE?

BEATS WALKING!

WIERD. THERE'S A NEW HOUSING DEVELOPMENT. I GUESS STUFF CHANGES WHEN YOU'VE BEEN AWAY FOR A YEAR AN' A HALF.

I CAN'T WAIT TO SEE MOM, DAD, GRAMPS AN' APRIL. I HAVE MISSED MY FAMILY SO MUCH!

ME, TOO.

MINE, I DON'T MISS.

PEOPLE CHANGE IN A YEAR AN' A HALF, CANDACE. YOUR MOM WILL PROBABLY TREAT YOU IN A TOTALLY DIFFERENT WAY.

YOU MEAN SHE WON'T YELL AT ME? SHE WON'T LET HER BOYFRIEND HIT ON ME? WE'LL BE, LIKE...PALS?

IF YOU FEEL LIKE THAT..., WHY ARE YOU HERE?

IT'S "HOME", LIZ.

MERRY CHRISTMAS.

WHAT'S THIS?

OUR HOLIDAY SCHEDULE.

WE HAVE A SCHEDULE?

WE'RE HAVING THE "BIG DINNER" WITH YOUR PARENTS, SO MY MOM WANTS US TO BE IN BURLINGTON ON THE 24TH

SHE WANTS US TO BE THERE ON THE MORNING OF THE 25TH BUT, YOUR PARENTS WANT US AT YOUR HOUSE TO OPEN GIFTS WITH APRIL —

SO, I THOUGHT I'D STAY OVER AT MY PARENT'S HOUSE, 'CAUSE MY SISTER WILL BE THERE AND YOU CAN DRIVE BACK TO THE CITY SO YOU CAN BE WITH YOUR FAMILY IN THE MORNING

THEN, I'LL BORROW MY DAD'S CAR, AND MEET YOU AROUND 3 SO WE CAN SPEND THE REST OF THE DAY AND HAVE — TURKEY DINNER AT YOUR PLACE THAT NIGHT.

ON THE MORNING OF THE 26TH, I'LL DRIVE BACK TO BURLINGTON AND SPEND SOME OF BOXING DAY WITH MY FAMILY....

AND YOU CAN PICK ME UP IN OUR CAR LATER!

:SIGH!:

WHAT?

I WAS JUST THINKING....

THIS IS OUR FIRST REAL CHRISTMAS **TOGETHER!**

Lynn

ELIZABETH! YOU'RE HERE!!

I LIKE SAVING THE BEAST FOR LAST!

WHERE'S GRANDPA, MOM? EVERYONE'S WAITING TO OPEN THEIR GIFTS!

HE HAD TO BRUSH AND PUT IN HIS TEETH, FIND HIS GLASSES, GET HIS CANE AND PUT A NEW BATTERY IN HIS HEARING AID.

OH

SORRY TO HOLD YOU ALL UP ON CHRISTMAS MORNING....

....AT MY AGE, I COME WITH "SOME ASSEMBLY REQUIRED!"

HERE WE ARE IN THE KITCHEN TOGETHER— JUST LIKE OLD TIMES!

YEAH!

ARE YOU ENJOYING SCHOOL? HAVE YOU MADE SOME GOOD FRIENDS? IS EVERY-THING OK?

OK.

ARE YOU HAPPY, ELIZABETH?

YEAH, I'M HAPPY! DON'T I LOOK HAPPY? WHAT MAKES YOU THINK I'M NOT HAPPY?

AAAAHH

AND... (SNIFF!) IT'S NOT THAT I DON'T TRUST ERIC, IT'S JUST THAT.... IT'S NOT PERFECT BETWEEN US. (SNIFFL!)

HE'S OUT WITH HIS FRIENDS ALL THE TIME AN' HE SAYS I'M TRYING TO "OWN" HIM—BUT, I'M NOT!

WHONK!

HE SAYS HE LOVES ME, AND I KNOW I LOVE HIM, BUT RIGHT NOW I'M BEGINNING TO WONDER WHAT LOVE REALLY IS!

HEY, SISTWIRP, DEANNA AND I ARE GOING OVER TO GORD'S GARAGE. WANNA COME?

SURE. WHY NOT.

THIS IS GREAT! WE HAVEN'T SEEN GORD AND TRACEY FOR AGES!

MMM

YOU GO IN FIRST, LIZ. YOU'VE CHANGED SO MUCH, I BET THEY WON'T RECOGNIZE YOU!!

ELIZABETH?

ANTHONY!!!

ELIZABETH... YOU LOOK.... AMAZING!

ANTHONY— WE CAME TO VISIT GORD AND TRACEY. I DIDN'T EXPECT TO SEE YOU HERE!

I'M WORKING ON THE BOOKS. THEY'VE GOT A PRETTY COMPLICATED BUSINESS GOING ON NOW, AND....

YOU HAVE A MOUSTACHE!

WOW! HERE I AM, TALKING TO THAT SWEET GUY I DATED IN HIGH SCHOOL!

I NEVER STOPPED THINKING ABOUT YOU, LIZ.

MIKE... DON'T YOU KNOW IT'S DANGEROUS TO LIGHT A FIRE IN A GAS STATION.

14

ELIZABETH, YOU'RE GOING OUT WITH ANTHONY?

UH HUH. WHAT'S WRONG WITH THAT?

OH, NOTHING! ... IT'S JUST NEW YEARS' EVE AN' YOU GUYS ARE SUPPOSED TO BE "INVOLVED" WITH OTHER PEOPLE

WELL, THE OTHER PEOPLE AREN'T HERE, APRIL— AND, BESIDES...

ANTHONY AND I HAVE KNOWN EACH OTHER SINCE WE WERE KIDS. WE'RE GOING OUT FOR "OLD TIME'S SAKE".

DING DONGGG!!

HEY, YOU! HEY YOURSELF!

YOU LOOK AMAZING SO DO YOU.

DID YOU SEE THAT? THOSE GUYS ARE, LIKE ALMOST ENGAGED TO OTHER PEOPLE, AN' THEY'RE DATING AGAIN!

MAN, THIS COULD WRECK THEIR OTHER RELATIONSHIPS!

WELL, IT'S THEIR BUSI-NESS, APRIL. WE KEEP OUR OPINIONS ENTIRELY TO OUR-SELVES

Lynn

15

ELIZABETH WENT WITH HER OLD BOYFRIEND TO A NEW YEARS' EVE PARTY?

A FANCY ONE, TOO!

THIS IS GOOD NEWS! I'VE ALWAYS LIKED ANTHONY AND THE BOY SHE'S WITH NOW, IS NO-THING BUT TROUBLE.

WELL, MAYBE, TONIGHT THE TWO OF THEM WILL EMBRACE AT MID-NIGHT, AND DISCOVER "THE TRUTH!"

OH, ANTHONY!! I WANTED YOU TO KNOW, LIZ.

HOW LONG HAVE YOU BEEN ENGAGED?

THREE WEEKS.

THESE ARE ALL MY DAD'S BUSINESS ASSOCIATES, LIZ. NO ONE WOULD MISS US IF WE LEFT!

WANT TO GO FOR A WALK?

SURE. I'D LIKE THAT.

I'LL PUT MY ARM AROUND YOU, TO KEEP YOU WARM.

I'D LIKE THAT, TOO.

ANTHONY, WHY DIDN'T YOU TELL ME YOU WERE ENGAGED?

WELL, WE SORT OF STOPPED WRITING TO EACH OTHER... DIDN'T WE.

THEN, YOU MOVED IN WITH ERIC, AND I STARTED DATING THÉRÈSE.

SHE MUST BE A WONDERFUL GIRL!

SHE IS.

IT'S TOO BAD SHE HAD TO GO BACK TO LONDON. I WANTED YOU TO MEET HER.

YES.

BUT, IT'S BEEN A GREAT EVENING. IT'S GIVEN US A WONDERFUL CHANCE TO CATCH UP!

AND, I WISH YOU'D NEVER STARTED RUNNING.

Panel 1: 2 AM! ELIZABETH SHOULD HAVE BEEN HOME BY NOW!

Panel 2: WHEN SHE'S AWAY AT SCHOOL, I DON'T WORRY—BUT WHEN SHE'S HERE, I WANT TO KNOW WHERE SHE IS ALL THE TIME!

Panel 3: WHAT'S KEEPING YOU AWAKE... MENOPAUSE?

NO,...

Panel 4: ...MOTHERHOOD.

Panel 5: CLICK, STEP, STEP, STEP.... WUFF! SHHHHHH

Panel 6: CANDACE?!!!!

THE DOOR WAS OPEN AN' THE LIGHT WAS ON. CAN I STAY HERE?

OF COURSE!

Panel 7: I THOUGHT YOU WERE ELIZABETH. SHE WENT TO A PARTY AND HASN'T COME HOME YET.

Panel 8: IF YOU'RE GOING TO STAY, WE'D BETTER CALL YOUR MOTHER AND TELL HER YOU'RE HERE!

DON'T BOTHER

Panel 9: SHE'S GONE TO A PARTY, AND HASN'T COME HOME, YET.

Panel 10: I HOPE YOU DON'T MIND SLEEPING ON THE REC-ROOM SOFA, CANDACE.

ANYWHERE'S FINE.

Panel 11: YOU'RE NOT GOING TO ASK WHY I SHOWED UP AT YOUR HOUSE IN THE MIDDLE OF THE NIGHT?

Panel 12: I DON'T LIKE TO PRY, HONEY. YOU HAVE YOUR REASONS, AND YOU'LL TELL ME WHEN YOU'RE READY.

Panel 13: (no dialogue)

Panel 14: I'M READY.

I'LL PUT THE COFFEE ON!

SO, I GET HOME AFTER BEING AWAY FOR A YEAR AN' A HALF. AT FIRST, MY MOM WAS SO HAPPY TO SEE ME, IT WAS GREAT.

BUT, WE STARTED ARGUING WHEN HER BOYFRIEND, LUKE, SHOWED UP. THE WAY HE LOOKS AT ME MAKES ME SICK.

I TRIED TO BE COOL, BUT HE KEPT GRABBING ME AND TOUCHING ME.

WHAT DID YOUR MOTHER SAY?!!

THAT IT NEVER HAPPENED.

AFTER CHRISTMAS, I SPENT A LOT OF TIME WITH FRIENDS. I SAW LIZ AN' DUANE AN' OTHER KIDS I KNOW.

BUT GOING HOME WAS AWFUL. I LOCKED MY DOOR AT NIGHT.

MOM AN' LUKE DECIDED TO GO TO A NEW YEAR'S EVE PARTY. I WENT OUT WITH DUANE, AND WHEN I GOT HOME, LUKE WAS THERE.

HE AN' MOM HAD A FIGHT. SHE STAYED AT THE PARTY, BUT HE CAME HOME. ...THEN HE CAME AFTER ME.

YOU DON'T HAVE TO SAY ANY MORE, CANDACE.

I COULDN'T THINK OF WHERE TO GO, SO I CAME HERE. —I KNOW IT'S A PAIN!

NO, HONEY... IT'S A COMPLIMENT!

ANTHONY, IT'S 4 O'CLOCK IN THE MORNING!

WHAT?

WE'VE BEEN TALKING ALL NIGHT!

THE TIME'S GONE SO FAST. I'D BETTER GET YOU HOME, OR PEOPLE ARE GOING TO THINK....

WHO CARES WHAT THEY THINK!

TWO GOOD FRIENDS HAD A WONDERFUL EVENING TOGETHER AND, IT'S BEEN NOTHING MORE THAN THAT.

GOOD NIGHT, ANTHONY.

GOODBYE, ELIZABETH.

CANDACE? HEY, LIZ. I HAD A FIGHT WITH MY MOM'S BOY-FRIEND, SO I'VE MOVED IN WITH YOU 'TIL WE GO BACK UP NORTH.

IT'S 5 IN THE MORNING! I KNOW, I SPENT ALL NIGHT TALKING TO YOUR MOM.

HOW WAS THE PARTY?

FOGEY, FANCY, FORMAL. MY "DATE" ANNOUNCED HE WAS ENGAGED.

ANTHONY CAINE IS ENGAGED? WHOA!!!!

WHY ARE YOU LOOKING AT ME LIKE THAT?!!

IT'S 5 O'CLOCK IN THE MORNING.

OK, YOU TWO — READY TO ROLL?

GRUNT

SNORT

YOU AREN'T GOING TO GET ON THE BUS LOOKING LIKE THAT, ARE YOU? — IT'S LIKE YOU JUST GOT OUT OF BED!

WE DID JUST GET OUT OF BED, DAD.

≋TSK≋ DON'T YOU WONDER WHAT THE OTHER PEOPLE ON THE BUS WILL THINK?

OH.

NORTH

ANOTHER 4 HOURS AN' WE'RE "HOME", LIZ.

YEAH. HOLIDAY'S OVER!

ORILLIA 10 KM

WHAT HOLIDAY? MY MOTHER'S BOYFRIEND IS A PERVERT. SHE SIDES WITH HIM AGAINST ME. I END UP AT YOUR PLACE. HAPPY NEW YEAR!

MY MOM STILL TREATS ME LIKE A KID.... AND I GO OUT WITH MY EX-BOYFRIEND WHO'S ENGAGED, BUT STILL LOVES ME.

I KNOW HE STILL LOVES ME, CANDACE ..... AND, I'M SO CONFUSED!

YEAH. (SIGH) LIFE WOULD BE SO EASY.... IF IT WASN'T FOR RELATIONSHIPS.

19

WHAPPP

JUST A MINUTE, GUYS!

I GOTTA GET NEW GLOVES.... THESE ONES ARE SOAKING!

APRIL! YOU LEFT THE FRONT DOOR WIDE OPEN! WE'RE NOT PAYING TO HEAT THE NEIGH-BORHOOD, YOU KNOW!

WHAT WAS THAT?

WHAT WAS WHAT?

YOU GAVE ME "THE LOOK"

WHAT "LOOK"?

YOU KNOW WHAT I MEAN...THE "OH,CHEEZ, NOT THIS AGAIN... GO STUFF A SOCK IN IT" KIND OF LOOK.

DON'T STAND THERE LIKE THAT!

LIKE WHAT?

WITH YOUR ATTITUDE!

WHAT "ATTITUDE"? I'M JUST STANDING HERE!

HOW ABOUT IF I LIE DOWN AND LOOK AT THE FLOOR, OK?

THAT DOES IT!

WHY DID YOUR MOTHER SEND YOU TO YOUR ROOM, APRIL?

....I LEFT THE FRONT DOOR OPEN.

LYNN

21

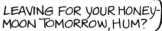

Panel 1:
LEAVING FOR YOUR HONEYMOON TOMORROW, HUM?
YEAH. DEANNA WANTED A DAY TO GET ORGANIZED.

Panel 2:
WE'RE HEADING FOR MONTRÉAL FIRST, THEN ON TO QUÉBEC CITY... THEN DOWN TO VERMONT FOR SOME SKIING.
COOL.

Panel 3:
WE COULD HAVE FLOWN SOMEWHERE, BUT DRIVING GIVES YOU THE OPPORTUNITY TO STOP ALONG THE WAY.
GOOD CALL.

Panel 4:
STOPPING MAKES ASKING FOR DIRECTIONS A WHOLE LOT EASIER.

Panel 5:
DEANNA? WHY ALL THE LUGGAGE? WE'RE ONLY GOING AWAY FOR TWO WEEKS!

Panel 6:
I DON'T WANT TO WEAR THE SAME THING EVERY DAY, MICHAEL. BESIDES— WE MIGHT GO TO SOME FANCY PLACES!
OH.

Panel 7:
WHAT DID YOU PACK FOR ME?
NOTHING, YET.
ZZZZZIP

Panel 8:
THESE ARE JUST MY SUITCASES!

Panel 9:
IS THAT ALL YOU'RE TAKING?
I'M ON HOLIDAY, DEE! I DON'T WANT TO DRESS UP!

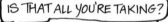

Panel 10:
I PACKED ONE GOOD OUTFIT, AND IF I REALLY NEED SOMETHING ELSE, WE CAN GO SHOPPING.

Panel 11:
I'VE GOT THE CAR READY— WHAT ARE YOU DOING?

Panel 12:
MAKING ROOM IN MY BAGS FOR NEW STUFF!

22

SO, THE ENGINE'S TUNED, TIRES CHECKED, TANK'S FULL — WE'VE GOT WINDOW WASHER FLUID, JUMPER CABLES AND EMERGENCY KIT.

SUITCASES ARE IN THE TRUNK, PHONE NUMBERS AND ADDRESSES ARE WITH OUR PARENTS AND WEED WILL WATER THE PLANTS.

WE HAVE PASSPORTS, CANADIAN AND U.S. CASH, WE ARE READY TO GO, WE HAVE FORGOTTEN NOTHING.

IF WE HAVE, IT'S NOTHING IMPORTANT.

...MAPS WOULD BE NICE.

MIKE AND DEANNA HAVEN'T CALLED YET. I WONDER WHERE THEY ARE.

BY NOW, THEY'LL BE IN QUÉBEC CITY.

BUT, WHAT ARE THEY DOING?

THEY'RE EXPLORING, GOING TO NICE CAFÉS — IT'S A HOLIDAY!!

THEY'LL BE TOO BUSY TO CALL! ...BESIDES, IT'S THEIR HONEYMOON. YOU KNOW VERY WELL WHAT THEY'RE DOING.

DOES THIS SUIT ME, HONEY, OR SHOULD I GET THE BLACK ONE?

NOUVEAUTÉS PRINTANIÈRES

WE NEVER DID HAVE A HONEYMOON, DID WE, JOHN.

WE'VE BEEN ON SOME NICE VACATIONS.

BUT, WE NEVER HAD WHAT ONE COULD CALL A REAL "HONEYMOON"!

WE COULDN'T AFFORD IT, EL.

STILL, A HONEYMOON WOULD HAVE BEEN SO NICE.

JUST A MINUTE....

WHAT'S THAT?

HONEY.

OH NO, YOU DON'T!

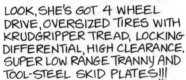

I FINALLY GOT A CALL FROM MIKE AND DE-ANNA. —THEY'RE IN VERMONT.

WHAT DO YOU MEAN, "FINALLY"?

I THOUGHT THEY'D HAVE CALLED ME SOONER!

WHY? THIS IS THEIR HONEYMOON!

THEY DON'T **HAVE** TO CALL HOME, CONNIE. I JUST LIKE THEM TO LET ME KNOW THAT EVERYTHING'S OK!

WHEN LAWRENCE TRAVELS, HE NEVER CALLS— AND I KNOW HE'S JUST FINE.

HOW?

IF HE WASN'T... HE'D CALL!

OUR KIDS ARE ADULTS, EL. WE HAVE TO LET GO!

I DON'T INTER-FERE IN THEIR LIVES, CONNIE!

BUT, YOU STILL LIKE TO KNOW WHAT THEY'RE DOING ALL THE TIME!

SO?

WHEN ARE YOU GOING CUT THOSE KIDS FROM THE PROVERB-IAL APRON STRINGS?

...WHEN THEY STOP COMING OVER TO RAID MY PROVERBIAL FRIDGE.

COMING IN FOR A COFFEE?

SURE. I'LL JUST TAKE THE DOGS HOME.

JOHN? DAD? APRIL?

YES? YAH? YES?

WHAPPITA-WHAP-ITA-WHAPPITA-WHAP!

...HERE

IF I WALK 'EM.... YOU WIPE 'EM!

STAND STILL, EDDY! DIXIE! STOP SHAKING!!

SO, IT'S A BRAND NEW YEAR. I WONDER WHAT'S IN STORE FOR US.

I'M GOING TO BE 50, FOR ONE THING!

I DON'T WANT TO BE 50, ELLY.

IT'S NOT SO BAD. I TURNED 50 LAST YEAR.

WHAT?!

YOU HAD YOUR 50TH BIRTHDAY, AND DIDN'T TELL ANY-ONE?

I DIDN'T FEEL LIKE CELEBRATING!

AT LEAST YOU COULD HAVE LET ME COME OVER AND BE MISERABLE WITH YOU.

I CAN'T BELIEVE YOU HAD YOUR 50TH BIRTH-DAY LAST YEAR, AND DIDN'T SAY ANY-THING!

JOHN KNEW, OF COURSE, BUT HE PROMISED NOT TO TELL. WE JUST WENT OUT AND HAD A QUIET DINNER TOGETHER.

WE TALKED ABOUT LIFE AND LOVE. I WANTED TO THINK ABOUT MY ACCOMPLISHMENTS ... AND ALL THE THINGS I HAVE YET TO ACCOMPLISH.

TURNING 50 IS A SOBERING EVENT, CONNIE.

I KNOW.

THAT'S WHY I PLAN TO GET BLASTED.

I'M NOT GOING TO BE LIKE YOU, EL. I'M GOING TO CELEBRATE MY 50TH BIRTHDAY!

I WANT ALL MY FRIENDS TO COME. I WANT A BIG PARTY WITH ALL THE GAG GIFTS, A CAKE, THE "OVER THE HILL" BALLOONS— THE WORKS!

I CAN'T TURN BACK THE CLOCK, SO I MIGHT AS WELL ACCEPT THE INEVITABLE.

I ADMIRE YOUR ATTITUDE, CONNIE.

THEN, I'M GOING TO HAVE A FACE LIFT, TUMMY TUCK AND LIPOSUCTION.

CONNIE'S ANNOYED WITH ME FOR NOT TELLING HER I TURNED 50 LAST YEAR.

I'M NOT SURPRISED.

I STILL DON'T KNOW WHY YOU WANTED TO KEEP IT A SECRET, EL. WE'RE ALL GETTING OLDER – AND I THINK YOU LOOK FINE.

CONNIE'S TALKING ABOUT HAVING LIPOSUCTION. DO YOU THINK I SHOULD HAVE LIPOSUCTION, JOHN?

DEFINITELY.

-SMAKK-

YO! IT'S THE RETURN OF THE HONEYMOONERS! – WHERE'D YOU GO, MIKE?

TO EVERY STORE BETWEEN QUEBEC CITY AND MONTPELIER, VERMONT.

NO SKIING? NO FANCY HOTELS WITH WHIRLPOOL TUBS?

YEAH, WE DID SOME OF THAT, WEED – BUT, MOSTLY, WE SHOPPED.

WHAT DID YOU BUY?

NOT MUCH. DEANNA JUST LIKES TO GO FROM STORE TO STORE AND LOOK AT STUFF. THAT'S HER IDEA OF A GREAT VACATION.

AND YOUR IDEA OF A GREAT VACATION?

... WE DID SOME OF THAT, TOO.

WAIT 'TIL YOU SEE THE PHOTOS OF OUR TRIP, JO- THE SCENERY WAS SPECTACULAR.

WHAT'S THIS?

THAT'S WHEN WE SLID OFF THE ROAD IN PORT- NEUF.

HERE'S THE GUY WHO PULLED US OUT... AND HERE'S HIS FAMILY!

LOOKS LIKE YOU'RE IN A KITCHEN.

IT HAPPENED NEAR HIS HOUSE, SO HIS WIFE INVITED US IN FOR LUNCH.

COOL!

... YOU MEET THE NICEST PEOPLE BY ACCIDENT!

MAN, HERE I AM, SHOWING SNAPSHOTS TO A PROFESSIONAL PHOTOGRAPHER!

I TAKE PICS LIKE THESE, TOO DEANNA!

THESE ARE A RECORD! YOU'RE NOT LOOKING AT LIGHTING AND COMPOSITION—YOU'RE LOOKING AT THEIR CONTENT!

PHOTOGRAPHS ARE A DIARY! THEY'RE ONE OF THE FIRST THINGS PEOPLE SAVE WHEN THERE'S A FIRE! PHOTOGRAPHS ARE SOME OF THE MOST PRECIOUS THINGS WE OWN.

I KNOW...

—THAT'S WHY WE'RE GOING TO START PUTTING THEM INTO ALBUMS, SOMETIME!

Photos 2001 1998 1999 2000

WHAT'S THIS, WEED?

I FIGURED YOU WOULDN'T HAVE TIME TO SHOP, SO I STOCKED YOUR FRIDGE.

WOW!

MILK, EGGS, FRUIT, CHEESE—WHAT DO WE OWE YOU?

NOTHING?

NADA.

JO, WE CAN'T LET YOU PAY FOR THIS!

CONSIDER IT A FAIR EXCHANGE.

WHILE YOU WERE GONE, I RENTED MY PLACE TO A GUY WHO NEEDED TO CRASH FOR 2 WEEKS.

—SO, I CHARGED HIM 400 BUCKS, AN' STAYED HERE!

A COUPLE OF GOOD JOBS CAME IN WHILE YOU WERE AWAY, MIKE. I GOTTA BRING YOU UP TO SPEED.

WANNA TALK HERE OR GO NEXT DOOR TO MY PLACE?

LET'S GO TO YOUR PLACE AND GIVE DEE SOME TIME TO HERSELF.

I'M COOL. WHAT YOU'RE SAYING IS—AFTER 2 WEEKS OF CONSTANT TOGETHERNESS, YOU NEED A BREAK FROM EACH OTHER!

WHAT HE'S SAYING IS... HE'S LEAVING ME TO UNPACK EVERYTHING AND CHECK THE MAIL.

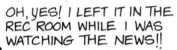

I'M GLAD THE MARRIAGE IS STILL IN TACT, MIKE. THAT MUCH TIME ALONE WITH A WOMAN WOULD FRY MY HEAD!

YOU JUST HAVEN'T FOUND THE RIGHT GIRL!

I'M NOT LOOKING, EITHER. I DON'T NEED COMMITMENTS, MAN.

MY LIFE'S THE WAY I LIKE IT. NOBODY TELLS ME WHAT TO DO OR WHEN TO DO IT.

WHAT'S THIS, WEEDER?

A WORK ORDER.

THIS JOB HAS TO BE IN BY FRIDAY OR THEY'LL BURN MY SHORTS... WHILE I'M WEARING THEM.

Lynn

GOT A CALL FROM THE MAGAZINE, MIKE.— THEY'VE LINED UP A SERIES OF INTERVIEWS AN' THEY WANT LOTS OF PICS!

THEY WANT YOU AN' ME TOGETHER ON THIS, AND THEY WANT AN ANSWER, LIKE— NOW!

GREAT.

THIS IS GONNA TAKE UP NIGHTS AND WEEK- ENDS.— I'M ALREADY WORKING FULL TIME FOR THESE GUYS, MAN!

BUT, IT'S GONNA PAY MEGA BUCKS! WE'RE TALKING ABOUT MONEY, SHAKESPEARE!

...WE USED TO TALK ABOUT "ART."

SO, LET'S TALK ABOUT THE ART OF MAKING MONEY!

Lynn

I TOLD YOU NOT TO TAKE A FULL TIME EDITING JOB, MIKE. YOU AN' I WERE DOING GREAT ON OUR OWN!

I COULDN'T GET MARRIED AN' DO FREELANCE, WEED.

WHY NOT? YOUR WIFE IS WORKING!

SHE'S COVERING FOR PEOPLE ON MATERNITY LEAVE! WE NEEDED MORE SECURITY!

I'M SAYING YOU'VE **GOT** SECURITY!

BEEEEEEEEEEE

TRUST ME, MAN — YOU CAN'T LET AN OPPORTUNITY GO UP IN SMOKE!

Lynn

BEEEEEEEEE

WE'RE SERIOUS PROFESSIONALS NOW, MAN! —WE COULD START OUR OWN BUSINESS!!

SNIFF? ...POO!!

WHAT HAPPENED? THERE'S A FIRE IN MY HOUSE?!!

BWAP!

I WAS FRYING UP AN EGG, MRS. SALTZMAN. I JUST FORGOT...

I HAVE TO TELL YOU THIS? —IF YOU'RE GOING TO COOK, WATCH WHAT IT IS YOU'RE COOKING! YOU COULD MAKE A CATASTROPHE WITH ONE EGG!!!

OY! I DON'T NEED SUCH EXCITEMENT! —WHY DO I RENT THIS PLACE TO KIDS?!!!

Lynn

HEY, IT'S THE BRUSHING BLIDE!

MRS. SALTZMAN SAID YOU SET OFF THE SMOKE ALARM, SO I CAME OVER...

WE'VE GOT A HOT CONVERSATION GOIN' DOWN HERE, GIRL! MIKE AN' I ARE ABOUT TO COLLABORATE ON ANOTHER BIG JOB FOR PORTRAIT MAGAZINE.

I'M TRYING TO TALK HIM INTO DUMPING THE FULL TIME GIG, AND GO INTO BUSINESS.

IT WOULD MEAN TAKING A FEW RISKS—

BUT, WEED AND I ARE FAIRLY WELL KNOWN NOW, DEE. WE COULD DO SOMETHING CRAZY!! —WHAT DO YOU THINK?!!

I THINK I'M PREGNANT.

PREGNANT?! —BUT, DEANNA—WHY DIDN'T YOU TELL ME WHILE WE WERE ON OUR TRIP?

I WASN'T SURE!

BESIDES, I WANTED TO SHOP AND SKI AND HAVE FUN! —I THOUGHT THE EXCITEMENT WAS UPSETTING MY STOMACH!

YOU WERE SICK?

BUT... NOW, I'M RELATIVELY SURE.

WHAT DO YOU MEAN... "RELATIVELY"?

IT MEANS YOU'RE EXPECTING A RELATIVE, MIKE...

THE KIND THAT TAKES 20 YEARS TO PACK UP AND GO HOME.

Lynn

IRIS, I'D LIKE TO BUY YOU A GIFT.... FOR VALENTINE'S DAY.

REALLY?

OH, JIM—HOW SWEET! DO YOU KNOW WHAT I'D REALLY LOVE TO HAVE?

A CELL PHONE!!!

A CELL PHONE?

I WAS THINKING ABOUT A FRIENDSHIP RING! A CELL PHONE IS SO UNROMANTIC!

NO, IT ISN'T!

WHEN YOU NEED A LITTLE FRIENDSHIP.... YOU CAN RING!!

33

DEANNA, HOW COULD YOU BE PREGNANT? —YOU'RE A PHARMACIST, FOR HEAVENS' SAKE!

I'M SORRY, MIKE.

I WANTED TO CHANGE MEDICATIONS, SO I WAITED FOR THE FIRST ONE TO LEAVE MY SYSTEM, AND... IT JUST HAPPENED!

BUT, WE STILL DON'T KNOW FOR SURE!

I JUST TOOK THE HOME PREGNANCY TEST...AND, IT'S POSITIVE.

MAY I SUGGEST A LITTLE COGNAC ON THIS MOMENTOUS OCCASION?

I CAN'T DRINK NOW, JO.

I WAS THINKING OF THE FATHER TO BE.

SHREIK!! A **BABY**?!! MICHAEL, THAT IS THE MOST WONDERFUL NEWS! I'M SO HAPPY FOR YOU!!!

OH, I KNOW YOU WEREN'T PREPARED—NOBODY'S PREPARED! EVEN PEOPLE WHO THINK THEY'RE PREPARED, AREN'T PRE-PARED!

YOU'RE GOING TO BE RESPONSIBLE FOR A NEW LIFE! YOU'RE GOING TO BE A FATHER! .... HONEY, WE ARE GOING TO HAVE MORE IN COMMON THAN WE'VE EVER HAD BEFORE!!

WHAT IS IT?

I THINK I JUST FELT A HAIR GO GREY.

I'M SO SORRY, MICHAEL.

YOU CAN'T TAKE ALL THE BLAME, DEE. I HAD A HAND IN IT, TOO ... SO TO SPEAK.

I HOPED WE COULD START A FAMILY IN A YEAR OR TWO. I NEVER THOUGHT...

WELL—THESE THINGS HAPPEN, I GUESS.

AT LEAST WE HAVE TIME TO ADJUST TO IT. —I WON'T BE DUE UNTIL OCTOBER.

BUT, ALL THESE BILLS ARE DUE NOW!

GET OUT!! I'M GONNA BE AN **AUNTIE**? WHEN?!!

NOVEMBER, LATE OCTOBER, MAYBE.

THAT IS SO TOTALLY SWEET!

AND, I'M GOING TO BE A GRANDMOTHER!

WHICH PUTS ME INTO THE "GREAT" CATEGORY.

ISN'T IT WONDERFUL, DAD? YOU'LL BE BOUNCING A GREAT GRANDCHILD ON YOUR KNEES!

I DON'T KNOW ABOUT THAT, DEAR...

NOWADAYS, THE ONLY THING I CAN BOUNCE ON THESE KNEES IS **ME**!

CONNIE! I'M GOING TO BE A GRANDMOTHER!

YOU'RE KIDDING!

NO, THEY ARE!

MIKE AND DEANNA ARE EXPECTING?

IT WAS A BIG SURPRISE FOR BOTH OF THEM... BUT, I AM SO EXCITED!!

CONGRATULATIONS, ELLY! – A FEW WEEKS AGO, YOU WERE GROUSING ABOUT BEING OVER 50. NOW, THE WRINKLES WON'T MATTER SO MUCH ANY MORE!

OH, THEY'LL MATTER...

THEY'LL JUST BE HIDDEN IN THE SMILES.!!!

WE'RE ACTUALLY GOING TO BE GRANDPARENTS, JOHN! – I CAN HARDLY WAIT.

THE KIDS ARE GOING TO HAVE A TOUGH TIME REORGANIZING THEIR LIVES TO ACCOMMODATE A BABY, EL.

THEY'LL BE FINE. AFTER ALL, THEY ONLY LIVE AN HOUR AWAY. I CAN HELP THEM WITH EVERYTHING!

I THOUGHT YOU SAID YOU WERE GOING TO BE THE KIND OF MOTHER IN LAW WHO WOULD NEVER INTERFERE IN YOUR ADULT CHILDRENS' LIVES.

I LIED.

CANDACE! GUESS WHAT! – I GOT AN E-MAIL THIS MORNING – AND I'M GONNA BE AN <u>AUNT</u>!

WHAT?

AN AUNT! MY BROTHER'S WIFE IS PREGNANT!

PLANNED OR ACCIDENT?

I DON'T KNOW. I THOUGHT THEY WERE GONNA WAIT AWHILE, BUT...

DEANNA'S A PHARMACIST, RIGHT?

SO?

SO... IT WAS A PLANNED ACCIDENT!

YOU'VE MET MY ROOM-MATE, RIGHT?

SURE! ANITA'S IN MY NATIVE STUDIES CLASS.

HI!

YOU'RE GOING TO BE A "TIA", ELIZABETH! – THAT'S "AUNT" IN SPANISH.

IN FRENCH, YOU'D BE "MA TANTE".

I'LL BE CALLED "AUNTIE ELIZABETH". I CAN'T WAIT!

BUT THIS WILL BE YOUR BROTHER'S KID, RE-MEMBER?

THAT MEANS YOU'LL BE "AUNTIE LIZARD BREATH"!

OVER MY DEAD BODY!

IT WILL HAPPEN.

IT'S GOOD THAT YOU'RE BACK IN SCHOOL, CANDACE.

YEAH! I SURE WAS LUCKY TO GET INTO RESIDENCE AGAIN.

ANITA'S A GOOD ROOMIE. SHE'S FROM MEXICO CITY. SOME DAY, I WANNA GO THERE WITH HER!

THAT'D BE SWEET!

HOW'S IT GOING WITH YOU AN' ERIC?

WE'RE WORKING THINGS OUT. I'M LEARNING TO BE LESS POSSESSIVE, AND MORE UNDERSTAND-ING.

AND, HE'S LEARNING?

THAT ONE MORE FALSE MOVE.... AN' I'M MOVING OUT.

HEY, BABE! SORRY, I'M LATE. I HAD TO SEE ONE OF THE T.A.'S ABOUT SOMETHING...

ERIC! GUESS WHAT!!

I'M GOING TO BE AN AUNTIE! MY BROTHER AND HIS WIFE ARE GOING TO HAVE A BABY! - I AM SO PUMPED, I CAN'T BELIEVE IT!!

ALL I CAN THINK ABOUT IS HOLDING MY NEWBORN NIECE OR NEPHEW IN MY ARMS!

COOL.

DO YOU WANT CHILDREN, ERIC?

UMM.. AFTER I GET A GOOD CAR, A CONDO, TOP OF THE LINE STEREO, COMPUTER AN' DO SOME TRAVELLING....

MAYBE.

I KNEW IT.... THAT MEANS "YES"!!!

GOOD GRUB, LIZ. - I'M GONNA RUN. I'VE GOT A HOCKEY PRACTICE.

HOCKEY?

YEAH. A BUNCH OF GUYS WANNA GET TOGETHER AN' FIRE A PUCK AROUND. WE GOT SOME ICE TIME DOWN AT THE ARENA TONIGHT.

DON'T WAIT UP. WE MIGHT HANG OUT FOR AWHILE LATER.

I'VE GOT AN ESSAY DUE, SO I'LL BE BUSY ANYWAY.

I'M SO PROUD OF MYSELF. I'M NOT QUESTIONING ERIC. IF HE SAYS HE'S PLAYING HOCKEY, THEN THAT'S WHERE HE IS!

HEY, MOM! MICHAEL TOLD ME THE GREAT NEWS! ISN'T IT EXCITING? WHEN'S DEANNA DUE? REALLY? - THAT'S CLOSE TO HALLOWE'EN!

DAWN! I'M GONNA BE AN AUNTIE! THAT'S RIGHT! MY UGLY BROTHER IS GONNA BE A **DAD**!!

SHAWNA MARIE? GUESS WHAT!

WHY DO THEY GIVE US SO MUCH HOMEWORK? - ONE CAN ONLY DO SO MUCH IN AN EVENING!

I JUST TALKED TO ELIZABETH, JOHN. SHE'S IN GOOD SPIRITS—AND, SO EXCITED ABOUT THE BABY!

GREAT NEWS!

WELL, LOOK AT THIS!— WE'VE BEEN INVITED TO CONNIE'S 50TH BIRTHDAY PARTY!

YEAH, SHE WANTS TO CELEBRATE

IT SAYS "JOIN WITH ME IN CELEBRATING MY 'COMING OF AGE.'"

WHAT DOES SHE MEAN, "COMING" OF AGE?

WE'RE OVER 50! ... IT'S ALREADY **HERE !!**

ELLY, JUST BECAUSE YOU KEPT YOUR 50TH A SECRET, DOESN'T MEAN WE CAN'T GO NEXT DOOR AND CELEBRATE CONNIE'S BIRTHDAY!

OH, I'LL GO. EVERY-ONE ACCEPTS THESE THINGS DIFFERENTLY. IF SHE WANTS TO SHOUT " I'M 50" TO THE WORLD, THAT'S FINE WITH ME.

I JUST WANTED A QUIET TIME ALONE, TO CONTEMPLATE MY PAST, MY PRESENT, MY FUTURE...

50 MEANS THAT MORE THAN HALF OF YOUR LIFE HAS GONE BY, JOHN!

I KNOW

AND, I BELIEVE THE BEST IS YET TO COME!

WHERE ARE MOM AN' DAD GOING, GRAMPA?

TO A BIRTHDAY PARTY FOR CONNIE, NEXT DOOR.—IT'S HER 50TH.

AHH, I REMEMBER THOSE DAYS. I COULD STILL PLAY TENNIS AND RIDE MY BIKE...

OH, TO BE AS YOUNG AS 50 ONCE MORE!

WIERD!

TO ME, ANYONE OVER 25 IS PRACTICALLY MUMMIFIED!

THE INVITATION SAID "NO GIFTS" BUT, I COULDN'T GO TO CONNIE'S 50TH WITHOUT BRINGING A LITTLE SOMETHING...

RINGG!

SURPRISE!

AAAGH!

CONNIE, THIS IS YOUR BIRTHDAY!

WE'RE NOT LETTING YOU GET AWAY WITH KEEPING YOURS A SECRET, EL—SO YOU'RE SHARING MINE!

I'LL GET YOU FOR THIS, CONNIE POIRIER.

WE'RE ONLY 50 EL... THERE'S PLENTY OF TIME!

Lynn

GREAT PARTY, GUYS!—WHAT A GOOD IDEA!

AND, NOW FOR THE CAKE!

FLAMINGOES? THERE'S ONE FOR EACH 10 YEARS, EL. LET'S TAKE A DEEP BREATH AND MAKE A WISH!

HAPPY 50TH BIRTH

WAIT, WAIT, WAIT!!! THERE'S ONE THING YOU CAN'T WISH FOR, AND THAT'S TO LOOK YOUNGER, OK? NOW, GO!!

HAPPY 50TH BIRTH

HAPPY 50TH BIRTHD

Lynn

THIS IS AMAZING, CONNIE! HALF THE NEIGHBORHOOD MUST BE HERE!

ANNIE—I'M SO GLAD YOU COULD COME.

WHAT HAPPENED TO STEVE?

OH—HE'S HOME WATCHING TELEVISION. THERE'S A BIG GAME ON... I HOPE YOU DON'T MIND.

OF COURSE NOT! HOW'S HE ENJOYING HIS RETIREMENT?

HE'S HAVING A WONDERFUL TIME.

AND, HOW ARE YOU ENJOYING HIS RETIREMENT?

.... DON'T ASK.

Lynn

EVER SINCE STEVE RETIRED, HE FOLLOWS ME AROUND THE HOUSE. EVERYWHERE I GO, HE GOES.

HE WATCHES ME COOK, HE CHECKS HOW I FOLD THE SHEETS. HE HAS TO FILL THE DISHWASHER "THE RIGHT WAY". HE'S REARRANGED THE FURNITURE....

I USED TO HAVE A ROUTINE. NOW, EVERYTHING I DO HAS TO BE QUESTIONED AND SCRUTINIZED!

HE NEEDS A HOBBY, ANNE.

HE HAS ONE. HE'S DRIVING ME CRAZY.

WHEN STEVE WAS ON THE ROAD, THINGS WERE HARD ENOUGH. SOMETIMES HE'D BE GONE FOR 2 OR 3 WEEKS AT A TIME.

THEN I GOT THE JOB AT THE HOTEL, AND LIFE WAS BETTER. THE KIDS WERE ALL GROWN UP, AND I HAD A CAREER TO THINK ABOUT.

NOW, HE'S HOME, AND I'M THE BREADWINNER. —IT'S LIKE WE'VE REVERSED ROLES!

ONLY, HE DOESN'T COOK, CLEAN, MEND OR DO THE LAUNDRY.

I HEAR YOU, ANNE. GREG WILL BE RETIRING FROM THE BANK SOON, AND I'M DREADING IT ALREADY.

WHY?

BECAUSE HIS ENTIRE FOCUS WILL TURN TO GOLF!

THAT'S OK, CONNIE. AT LEAST HE'LL BE BUSY.

YOU DON'T UNDERSTAND, ELLY. — HE WATCHES GOLF VIDEOS, HE PRACTICES HIS SWING FOR HOURS. HE PUTTS IN THE HALLWAYS, HE'S BOUGHT EVERY CONCEIVABLE "LEARNING" CONTRAPTION AVAILABLE! — AND... HE'LL WANT ME TO PARTNER WITH HIM!!

SO?

.... I'M BETTER THAN HE IS.

HOW ABOUT YOU, EL. IS JOHN PLANNING TO GIVE UP HIS PRACTICE?

HE THINKS ABOUT IT, BUT I'M NOT WORRIED.

WELL, HANG ONTO YOUR BUSINESS DOWNTOWN. IT'S NOT EASY HAVING A RETIRED HUSBAND AROUND.

THEY DON'T KNOW WHAT TO DO WITH THEMSELVES! MEN NEED A CAREER. THEY HAVE TO BE CHALLENGED, THEY NEED A PURPOSE OR THEIR BRAINS ATROPHY.

I WONDER WHAT THOSE 3 ARE DISCUSSING SO SERIOUSLY!

OH... JUST "GIRL TALK".

WELL, I'LL BE TAKING EARLY RETIREMENT FROM THE BANK NEXT YEAR, JOHN—AND, I CAN'T WAIT!

IF I CAN GET CONNIE TO GIVE UP HER JOB AT THE HOSPITAL—OR TAKE A LEAVE OF ABSENCE... I'D LIKE TO TAKE A GOLFING TOUR! GO DOWN TO THE STATES, HIT A FEW PLACES IN FLORIDA...

I'M GEARING UP! SPENT MOST OF THE WINTER WORKING ON MY SWING AN' MY STANCE.—HOW'S YOUR GAME, NEIGHBOR?

NOT BAD, GREG—

I CAN FINALLY GET THE BALL TO GO FARTHER THAN MY DIVOTS!

THAT WAS A GREAT PARTY, CONNIE!

HAPPY 50TH!

YOU TOO, ELLY!

THANKS, CONNIE. I'M SO GLAD YOU GOT EVERYONE TOGETHER.

WE HAVE A NICE BUNCH OF FRIENDS.

TOO BAD WE NEED A REASON LIKE THIS. TIME'S GOING BY SO FAST...WE'RE ALL AT THE SAME STAGE OF OUR LIVES!

WE'RE ALL IN THE SAME BOAT.

WE NEED EACH OTHER NOW, MORE THAN EVER.

...TO HELP PLUG THE LEAKS!

HOW WAS YOUR CHECK UP THIS MORNING?

EVERYTHING'S FINE, MICHAEL. WE SHOULD HAVE A HEALTHY BABY.

ARE YOU O.K. ABOUT THIS?

SURE. IT'S JUST THAT I'D BEEN THINKING OF GIVING UP MY FULL TIME JOB AND GOING BACK TO FREE-LANCE.

BUT... A FAMILY NEEDS A STEADY INCOME.

THE WORD "FAMILY" SOUNDS SO DIFFERENT NOW, DOESN'T IT.

YEAH...

I'M STILL TRYING TO GET MY HEAD AROUND THE WORD "MARRIED"!

THE GIRLS AT WORK WERE SO EXCITED WHEN I TOLD THEM I WAS PREGNANT, MICHAEL.

WE'RE MOSTLY YOUNG WOMEN IN THE PHARMACY, SO THERE'S ALWAYS SOMEONE GOING ON MATERNITY LEAVE AND SOMEONE COMING IN TO REPLACE THEM!

MMM—

SOUNDS LIKE A REVOLVING DOOR! HOW DOES YOUR SUPERVISOR COPE WITH ALL THIS?

OH... SHE'S HAVING A TOUGH TIME RIGHT NOW.

SHE'S JUST HAD TWINS!

DO I SHOW YET?

I DUNNO... YOU JUST HAD DINNER.

THERE'S A DIFFERENCE BETWEEN "STOMACH BULGE" AND "BABY", MICHAEL. WHAT I WANT TO KNOW IS - DO I LOOK PREGNANT OR DO I LOOK FAT?!!

DEANNA, YOU DEFINITELY LOOK PREGNANT.

DINGGGGG!

YES!! THAT IS THE RIGHT ANSWER!

JAKPOT!

WE HAVE SOME PAPERS TO FILL OUT ABOUT THE ROBBERY.

LET'S GO DOWN TO THE OFFICE.

BRAD LUGGSWORTH! YOU LOOK JUST GREAT!

YEAH!-I'M MARRIED, HAVE TWO KIDS, GOT A JOB I ENJOY...

HOW'S MICHAEL?

HE'S MARRIED-AND THEY'RE EXPECTING THEIR FIRST BABY IN...

EXCUSE ME-

WE'LL NEED THE MANUFACTURER'S SPECS ON THE MODEL TRAIN ENGINE THAT WAS STOLEN.

SURE!

WELL, OFFICER LUGGSWORTH, I CAN'T TELL YOU WHAT A PLEASURE THIS HAS BEEN !!

I THINK WE HAVE ALL THE INFORMATION WE NEED, MRS. PATTERSON.

WE'LL BE IN TOUCH.

THANKS FOR YOUR HELP.

DID YOU KNOW THAT OFFICER, ELLY?

HE WENT TO SCHOOL WITH MY SON. IT WAS NICE TO SEE HIM AGAIN.

WHERE'S KORTNEY, MOIRA?

I DON'T KNOW. I HAVEN'T SEEN HER FOR THE LAST HALF HOUR!

KORTNEY?

IT'S ALL MY FAULT! I LEFT THE TRAIN CASE UNLOCKED AN' NOW, YOU'RE GONNA **FIRE** ME! ~SNIVEL'!!!

SOMETIMES, I FEEL MORE LIKE A PARENT THAN AN EMPLOYER!

KORTNEY, I'M NOT GOING TO FIRE YOU.

SNIFFF! ~FWONK~

WHAT HAPPENED WAS A LESSON, OK?- ALWAYS MAKE SURE THE DISPLAY CABINETS ARE LOCKED- EVEN IF YOU'RE GONE FOR A FEW MINUTES.

OK.

WE STILL HAVE 2 HOURS BEFORE THE SHOP CLOSES, SO LET'S GET BACK TO WORK.

WORK?!!

YOU MEAN I DON'T GET ANY TIME OFF FOR "STRESS LEAVE"?!!

WHO CALLED, LIZ?

MY DAD. SOMEBODY STOLE A LITTLE BRASS ENGINE FROM OUR STORE. MOM'S PRETTY UPSET.

TOO BAD! – WELL, I GOTTA GO.

YOU'RE GOING OUT AGAIN?

HOCKEY PRACTICE, LIZ – GOT A GAME COMIN' UP. – CAN'T LET THE GUYS DOWN.

ERIC, WAIT!

TELL ME LATER, OK? THIS IS IMPORTANT.

YOU FORGOT YOUR SKATES!

THERE'S A CAB PULLING UP TO THE APARTMENT! I BET I CAN GET DOWN TO THE ARENA BEFORE ERIC DISCOVERS HE'S FORGOTTEN HIS SKATES!

TAXI!

ARENA ENTRANCE

JASON! TELL ERIC I'VE GOT HIS SKATES!

I WOULD, LIZ BUT, HE'S NOT HERE.

WHAT? HE SAID HE HAD A PRACTICE! HE SAID THERE WAS A GAME COMING UP!

IF ERIC'S PLAYING GAMES, LIZ... IT ISN'T HOCKEY.

ARE YOU OK, ELIZABETH?

YEAH – WHAT DO YOU KNOW ABOUT ERIC, GUYS? WHAT'S GOING ON?

WE'RE NOT SURE. HE CAME TO A COUPLE OF PRACTICES WITH A GIRL CALLED TINA.

I KNOW TINA.

THEN, AFTER THE PRACTICE, THEY'D TAKE OFF SOMEPLACE.

I THINK I KNOW WHERE.

KNOCK, KNOCK, KNOCK, KNOCK...

HEY, ELIZABETH! WHAT'S UP?

I'M LOOKING FOR ERIC. IS HE HERE?

YEAH...

TELL HIM I WENT TO THE ARENA TO TAKE HIM HIS SKATES. TELL HIM I FOUND OUT HE WAS COMING TO YOUR PLACE INSTEAD OF GOING TO PRACTICES.

TELL HIM I KNOW HE'S A TWO-FACED LIAR!

WHAT ARE YOU TALKING ABOUT?

TAKE A GOOD LOOK AT HIM, TINA... AND FIGURE IT OUT.

ERIC, YOU DIRTBALL HAVE YOU BEEN CHEATING ON ME?!!!

TINA, ELIZABETH, JUST CALM DOWN, OK? YOU'RE ACCUSING ME OF STUFF AN' I NEED TO GET MY HEAD AROUND IT!

GET YOUR HEAD AROUND THIS!

ELIZABETH CALLED ONE NIGHT, LOOKING FOR YOU —AND, YOU TOLD ME TO SAY YOU WEREN'T HERE!

YOU HAD SOME STUPID REASON, AND LIKE AN IDIOT—I BELIEVED YOU!—YOU WERE CHEATING ON HER!

I KNEW YOU WERE HERE. I KNEW IT!

WHAT IS THIS? AM I ON TRIAL HERE? DON'T I GET TO SAY ANYTHING?

YES!

PLEAD GUILTY!!

ERIC, YOU COWARD! COME OUT OF THAT BATHROOM!!

GULP!

YOU SAID ELIZABETH WAS JUST A ROOM MATE! YOU SAID SHE JUST RENTED SPACE IN YOUR APARTMENT!

YOU SAID THERE WAS NOTHING BETWEEN YOU AND TINA, BUT THERE **IS**—ISN'T THERE!!!

...RIGHT NOW, IT'S A THIN DOOR AND A CHEAP BOLT LOCK!!

53

ELIZABETH, I TOTALLY HAD NO IDEA YOU AND ERIC WERE LIVING TOGETHER.

WHEN I STAYED THERE AT CHRISTMAS, HE SHOWED ME YOU HAD SEPARATE ROOMS, SO...

YOU STAYED AT OUR PLACE?!!

NO WONDER IT WAS SO CLEAN.

HE SAID HE WAS UNATTACHED.

OH, HE'S GOING TO BE UNATTACHED, ALL RIGHT!

—THERE'S GONNA BE PIECES OF HIM ALL OVER THIS APARTMENT!!!

OK! I GIVE UP! DON'T BREAK DOWN THE DOOR. I'M COMING OUT. —JUST GIVE ME A CHANCE TO EXPLAIN!!

THE REASON I WAS SEEING YOU BOTH IS BECAUSE ... I ... COULDN'T HELP MYSELF!! YOU'RE BEAUTIFUL AND BRILLIANT AND EXCITING AND... I'M COMPLETELY HOPELESSLY IN LOVE WITH BOTH OF YOU!!

I ... (SNIFF) NEVER MEANT TO HURT YOU.

ENOUGH, TINA—I'VE HAD ENOUGH!

GET YOUR BUTT OUTTA MY APARTMENT OR I'LL CUSTOMIZE YOUR FACE!

I'M LEAVING. WHERE ARE MY HOCKEY SKATES, LIZ?

IN THE SALVATION ARMY PICK UP BOX ON McINTYRE STREET.

WHAT?! YOU GAVE THEM TO **CHARITY?** BUT, THEY WERE BRAND NEW!!!

I KNOW.

I FIGURED SOMETHING GOOD HAD TO COME OUT OF THIS EVENING.

I'M REALLY SORRY, ELIZABETH. I HAD NO IDEA.

I'M NOT BLAMING YOU, TINA.

I GUESS I KNEW THAT ERIC WAS CHEATING ON ME. I JUST HAD TO SEE IT FOR MYSELF.

WHEN I FOUND HIM HERE AT YOUR APARTMENT, I BET HE THOUGHT YOU AND I WOULD HAVE A REAL "CAT FIGHT"!

YEAH....

BUT, YOU KNOW WHAT? ... A GUY LIKE ERIC ISN'T WORTH BREAKING A NAIL OVER!

WHAT ARE YOU GONNA DO NOW?

I THINK I'LL GO CRASH AT A FRIEND'S PLACE.. THEN TRY AND FIND SOMEWHERE ELSE TO LIVE.

STRANGE. I'VE JUST LOST MY APARTMENT AND BROKEN UP WITH A GUY I LOVED, AND I FEEL ABSOLUTELY NOTHING.

KNOCK, KNOCK!

ELIZABETH?

HI, RUBY.

RUBY, I'M SORRY TO WAKE YOU UP. I KNOW IT'S LATE.

HON, YOU'RE WELCOME HERE ANY TIME. 24-7

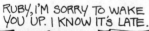

I KNOW THIS IS ABOUT ERIC, SO YOU SIT DOWN, HAVE A REAL GOOD CRY.... AND I'LL FIX US A DRINK.

WHY DID HE CHEAT ON ME, RUBY? I FEEL LIKE I'VE BEEN "THROWN AWAY"! I'M NOT STUPID OR UGLY OR SELFISH OR DULL. I'M TIDY AND CLEAN. I COOK, PAY MY OWN WAY. I'M HONEST, I'M CONSIDERATE I'M OPEN MINDED I'M FORGIVING I WORK HARD....

WHAT'S WRONG WITH ME?!!

RRRINGG!

YANK!!!

KLONK!

56

HE WAS SO SMOOTH, RUBY. TINA WORKS IN TOWN, AND ONLY CALLED HIM ON HIS CELL PHONE.

SHE BELIEVED ERIC AN' I WERE JUST ROOM MATES, AND I BELIEVED HE WAS EITHER AT SCHOOL OR WORKING OR AT HOCKEY PRACTICE ... WHEN HE WAS WITH HER!

HOW COULD TINA AND I BE SO **STUPID?**

WAIT A MINUTE!

ERIC JUST LOST THE RESPECT OF TWO TRUSTING PEOPLE. — HOW STUPID IS **THAT**?!!

KNOW WHAT ROTS MY SOCKS, LIZ? — SOME CLOD TREATS YOU LIKE YESTERDAY'S TOAST... AND, YOU GO 'ROUND BLAMING YOURSELF!!!

WHAT COULD I HAVE DONE TO MAKE HIM **LOVE** ME?!!

THE TRUTH IS — ABSOLUTELY NOTHING! A JERK IS A JERK. PERIOD.

I STILL FEEL LIKE SUCH A LOSER.

YOU'RE NOT A LOSER, MY DEAR... YOU ARE NOW A "WOMAN WITH EXPERIENCE."

YOU DON'T MIND IF I STAY HERE TONIGHT?

I'VE GOT A BED ALL MADE UP!

BUT, FIRST, YOU'RE GOING TO WASH YOUR FACE, COMB YOUR HAIR AND LOOK IN THE MIRROR.

SEE? YOU'RE A BEAUTY! AND, SOME DAY YOU'LL FIND A REAL LOVE THAT WILL LAST.

HOW DO YOU KNOW?

HONEY, MEN ARE LIKE WET FIREWORKS. JUST WHEN YOU THINK THEY'RE ALL DUDS.... YOU PICK UP A GOOD ONE!

WHAT? YOU DID?!! WELL, THAT'S GREAT NEWS!
THEY FOUND THE BRASS ENGINE?

ELIZABETH BROKE UP WITH HER BOY-FRIEND!
OH.

SORRY, HONEY. I DIDN'T MEAN TO SOUND SO HAPPY. I'M JUST GLAD YOU..... I JUST WANT WHAT'S BEST FOR....

UH-HUH...UM HMMM. UH-HUH, UH-HUH, MMM
MOM, IS THAT ALL YOU CAN SAY?!!!

THIS IS ONE OF THOSE MOTHER-DAUGHTER CONVERSATIONS, WHERE NO MATTER WHAT YOU SAY — IT'S THE WRONG THING.

WAS THAT ELIZABETH ON THE PHONE? — SHE USUALLY SENDS E-MAILS!
NOT WHEN SHE'S UPSET. THEN, SHE LIKES TO TALK PERSON TO PERSON.

REALLY? HOW COME?
WHEN SHE'S MISERABLE, SHE CALLS ME. THE CONVERSATION GETS COMPLICATED AND THEN **I'M** MISERABLE.

WOW! — IT'S LIKE A TRANSFER OF ENERGY! THAT IS SO COOL !!!

TAKING A BATH?
NO... I'M DISCHARGING.

CAN'T SLEEP?
I'M WORRIED ABOUT ELIZABETH.
SHE'LL BE FINE.

BUT, SHE DOESN'T HAVE AN APARTMENT, NOW.
SCHOOL'S ALMOST OVER. SHE CAN BUNK IN WITH FRIENDS.

BUT, SHE'S GOT FINAL EXAMS AND TERM PAPERS!
SHE'S AN ADULT. SHE'LL MANAGE.

HOW CAN YOU BE SO CAVALIER? AREN'T YOU THE LEAST BIT WORRIED?
NO.

... YOU ALWAYS WORRY ENOUGH FOR BOTH OF US.

58

MOM! CHECK IT OUT! — THERE'S A POLICE CAR OUTSIDE!

THERE'S A POLICEMAN, HE'S IN UNIFORM.... AN' HE'S COMING UP TO OUR DOOR!

WOW, THIS IS SO TOTALLY COOL!!!

DINGGG DONGGG..

— YOU ANSWER IT.

OFFICER LUGGSWORTH! PLEASE, COME IN.

JUST CALL ME "BRAD" NOW, MRS PATTERSON.

THE "OFFICER" BIT SOUNDS TOO FORMAL.

WE FOUND YOUR BRASS TRAIN ENGINE. WE JUST NEED YOU TO COME DOWN TOWN TO IDENTIFY IT, FILL IN SOME PAPERS AND LOOK AT SOME PHOTOGRAPHS.

DO THEY KNOW WHO STOLE IT?

WE HAVE FINGERPRINTS, A POSITIVE I.D. FROM THE PAWNSHOP WHERE IT WAS SOLD, WE'VE EVEN GOT A RECEIPT OUT OF THEIR CAR — SO, WE KNOW WHO DID IT, ALL RIGHT!

... WE JUST NEED MORE PROOF.

RECOGNIZE ANY OF THESE PHOTOGRAPHS, MA'AM?

YES. THIS IS DEFINITELY THE MAN WHO WAS TALKING TO ME AT THE COUNTER, AND I'M SURE THIS IS THE OTHER ONE.

IN FACT THEY'RE WEARING THE SAME CLOTHES THEY WORE WHEN THEY ROBBED THE STORE!

WHY WOULD THEY DO THAT?

WELL, WHEN YOU'RE IN AND OUT OF JAIL AS OFTEN AS THESE GUYS ARE, WHY BOTHER CHANGING!

OH, MAN, WE'RE GONNA BE LATE ON THE PHONE PAYMENT!

AND, THE CAR'S DUE FOR A TUNE-UP.

WE SPENT THE CHEQUE YOUR AUNT SENT US WHEN WE PAID BACK MY DAD.

AND, I WON'T GET PAID FOR THAT ARTICLE I WROTE FOR 60 DAYS!

WE COULD CASH IN A TERM DEPOSIT.

NO WAY!

WE HAVE TO DO SOMETHING, MICHAEL! —HOW **ELSE** CAN WE MAKE ENDS MEET?!

HEY!—YOU ASKED THE QUESTION!

THAT WASN'T THE ANSWER!

WHAT'S THE MATTER, HONEY?

I DUNNO. I JUST CAN'T SLEEP. I WONDER IF THIS IS PART OF BEING PREGNANT.

I TOSS AND TURN AND CAN'T GET COMFORTABLE. I FEEL RESTLESS AND IRRITABLE. MAYBE IT'S HORMONES OR SOMETHING.

I'M SORRY I'M KEEPING YOU AWAKE, MICHAEL.

THAT'S OK. AS LONG AS WE'RE BOTH UP, MAYBE I'LL GET SOME WORK DONE.

SORRY! I KNOW I'M LATE THIS MORNING!

BUT, I GOT THIS INTERVIEW DONE AND EDITED THE FREELANCE SUBMISSIONS.

I ALSO OUTLINED AN ARTICLE FOR RESEARCH AND MADE SOME FALL STORYLINE SUGGESTIONS.

YOU DID THIS ALL AT HOME?

WELL, I WAS UP AT 3 A.M., SO I THOUGHT I'D MAKE USE OF MY TIME.

THAT'S COMMENDABLE, MIKE!

IT'S NICE TO BE YOUNG! .... IF I'D BEEN UP SINCE 3, I'D BE A BASKET CASE BY NOW!!!

I BROUGHT IN SOME PIX, MIKE.

HEY, WEED.

YOU'VE GOT THAT "CAFFEINE STARE", MAN.

I'M NOT SLEEPING MUCH.

I THOUGHT DEANNA WOULD GET RESTLESS AND START PACING AROUND WHEN SHE WAS DUE BUT, SHE'S UP ALMOST EVERY NIGHT, AND WE HAVE 6 MORE MONTHS LEFT TO GO!

LAST NIGHT, I WAS CLEANING UP A PLATE OF CRACKERS AND SARDINES AT 4 IN THE MORNING!

WOW, SHE HAS CRAVINGS?

NO...

—I DO.

HELLO, MRS. SALTZMAN! COME IN.

JOSEF SAYS YOU DON'T SLEEP WELL, SO I MADE YOU SOME SOUP.

IT'S CHICKEN BROTH. YOU'LL LIKE IT.

THANK YOU!

AND, CALL ME "LOVEY". MY REAL NAME IS OLIVIA.—AFTER THE ACTRESS "OLIVIA DE-HAVILLAND".

OH?

OLIVIA IS A NICE NAME.

IT IS IF YOU LOOKED LIKE AN "OLIVIA"

BUT, I LOOKED MORE LIKE A DEHAVILLAND.

ARE YOU EATING? YOU LOOK THIN. YOU SHOULD EAT MORE.

I'M FINE, MRS. SALTZMAN.

CALL ME "LOVEY".

MY DAUGHTER, I TOLD WHEN SHE WAS PREGNANT, SHE SHOULD BE CAREFUL WHAT SHE EATS. SHE NEVER ATE ENOUGH GREENS. GREENS ARE GOOD.

YOU HAVE A GOOD DOCTOR? YOU'RE GETTING EXERCISE?

I THINK I'M DOING ALL THE RIGHT THINGS.

I'M GLAD TO HEAR IT. A "NEW MOTHER" HAS OBLIGATIONS!

— ONE OF WHICH IS TO LISTEN TO THE "OLD" ONES!!

HI, HONEY! HOW ARE YOU FEELING?

MUCH BETTER. I'M GLAD I HAD THE DAY OFF. I WAS ABLE TO GET SOME SLEEP.

MRS. SALTZMAN CAME BY A COUPLE OF TIMES.

REALLY?.. (SNIFF) WHAT'S COOKING?!

SHE BROUGHT US A CASSEROLE. IT'S STUFFED CABBAGE.

MMM—WHAT'S IT STUFFED WITH?

ADVICE.

PLASTIC SURGERY DISASTER AS IMPLANT FERMENTS.

SCANDAL ROCKS THE ROYALS

PREGNANT MUMMY FOUND IN TEMPLE RUINS! VISION OF ELVIS APPEARS ON TORTILLA! MALL RAGE SUSPECT BLAMES DEODORANT.

STAR SLAMS FOUR PRODUCERS WITH PATERNITY SUITS. PSYCHIC HEARS CODED MESSAGE COME FROM BOXER SHORTS. IDENTICAL TWINS SUE PARENTS OVER NEED FOR NOSE REDUCTION SURGERY. DOG EATS 12 FT. BUNGY CORD...

SCIENTISTS GENETICALLY COMBINE GOAT AND AVOCADO! CHEESE BLAMED FOR GAS EXPLOSION. STRIP-STAR DEVELOPS ALLERGY TO DUCT TAPE. WOODEN SPLINT CURES E.D.

ERIC! YOU WEREN'T SUP-POSED TO BE HERE!

SORRY, BABE. I JUST WANTED TO SAY GOODBYE.

I WANT MY COOK WARE BACK—AND I WANT MY SHOWER CURTAIN.

WITH PLEASURE! YOU KNOW I'M A PRETTY EASY GOING GUY.

WELL, ERIC, I'M A PRETTY EASY-GOING GIRL.

YEAH?!

I'M GOING .... AND, IT'S EASY.

ON YOUR WAY HOME?

UH HUH. I'VE GOT MY OLD JOB BACK AT THE SUPER-MARKET.

WHEN DOES YOUR BUS LEAVE?

IN 45 MINUTES, BUT IT'S OK. I ALREADY HAVE A TICKET.

IT WAS NICE OF YOU TO HELP ME WITH MY STUFF.

HEY—NO PROBLEM.

THANK HEAVENS I'VE FINALLY LEARNED HOW TO PACK!

I'M GOING HOME. I HAVEN'T LIVED WITH MY FAMILY FOR SO LONG!

I'M GOING BACK TO MY OLD ROOM, WITH ALL MY JUNK AND MY KIDDIE TOYS STILL IN THE CLOSET.

I'LL HEAR DAD GET-TING UP IN THE MORNING, MOM PUTTING ON THE COFFEE, APRIL AND THE DOGS THUMPING AROUND THE HOUSE.

HOME. WHERE I GREW UP. THE ONE PLACE THAT HASN'T CHANGED. THE ONE TRUE CONSTANT IN MY LIFE!

... I HOPE I CAN STAND IT FOR A WHOLE SUMMER!

SNARR!

SNARR!

DOES DIXIE "DO ANYTHING", JIM?

SURE, SHE GETS ME MY SLIPPERS.

DIXIE, GIRL! SLIPPERS! GO GET ME MY SLIPPERS!!

PANT, PANT, PANT

WHAPPITA-WHAPPITA-WHAPP

THIS IS IMPRESSIVE. SHE ACTUALLY BRINGS YOU YOUR SLIPPERS!

YES.

I DON'T ASK HER TO DO IT TOO OFTEN, THOUGH.

FOR GOODNESS SAKE! —WHY NOT?!!

... SHE LIKES TO CHEW THEM, FIRST.

DAD? DID YOU KNOW THAT GORDON'S GOT A NEW ICE CREAM FREEZER AT THE GAS STATION?

THERE'S CARAMEL AN' VANILLA WITH MILK CHOCOLATE, BIG DRUMSTICKS, TOFFEE AN' MARSHMALLOW BARS AN' TWO KINDS OF ESKIMO PIES!

HI THERE, GORD!

HEY, DR. P! IS THERE ANYTHING I CAN DO FOR YOU?

SURE!

...FILL 'ER UP!

ELIZABETH COMES HOME TODAY, GORDON! WE'RE GOING TO THE BUS STATION. SHE'S STAYING FOR THE WHOLE SUMMER!

SHE'S GOT HER JOB BACK AT MEGAFOOD, BUT SHE BROKE UP WITH HER BOYFRIEND FIRST AN' MOVED OUT OF THEIR APARTMENT, AN' MOM'S GLAD!

GRAMPA MIGHT BE MOVING SOON. I'M GONNA ENROLL IN MUSIC CAMP, EDGAR ATE A TOAD AN' THREW UP IN THE KITCHEN WHILE MOM WAS HAVING A CANDLE PARTY.

WOW!

APRIL TAKES HER NEWS DELIVERY FROM HOT-ROCK RADIO.

HOW'S BUSINESS, GORD?

PRETTY GOOD. WE BOUGHT THE PROPERTY NEXT DOOR IN CASE WE EXPAND AGAIN.

N'S GARAGE
ULL SERVICE

RIGHT NOW, WE'RE USING IT TO SHOWCASE SOME OF OUR PRE OWNED VEHICLES, AND I THINK I'LL MODIFY AND MOVE THE DETAILING SERVICE INTO THE BUILDING THAT'S THERE.

MOM DETAILED HER CAR LAST WEEK.

OH?

...SHE BACKED INTO A CEMENT POST AT THE MALL

69

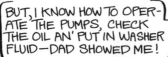

WHAT YOU'VE DONE IS IMPRESSIVE, GORD!
COULD I WORK FOR YOU THIS SUMMER?
SORRY, APRIL. YOU'RE TOO YOUNG.

BUT, I KNOW HOW TO OPERATE THE PUMPS, CHECK THE OIL AN' PUT IN WASHER FLUID—DAD SHOWED ME!

I STILL CAN'T HIRE YOU. I'D PROBABLY BE ARRESTED!
REALLY?

NO, APRIL. MAKING YOU SHOVEL OUT YOUR ROOM DOES NOT VIOLATE THE CHILD LABOR LAWS.

I WISH I WAS OLDER.
EVERYONE YOUR AGE WANTS TO BE OLDER, APRIL.

YOU WANT TO BE OLDER UNTIL YOU'RE ABOUT 25. AFTER THAT, YOU BEGIN TO EVALUATE YOURSELF.

YOU START TO TAKE THINGS MORE SERIOUSLY. YOU WONDER IF YOU'RE MAKING THE RIGHT CHOICES, FOLLOWING THE RIGHT PATHS...

AT 25, YOU LOOK YOUTHFUL, BUT YOUR MIND IS MATURE. IT'S A WONDERFUL AGE. ALL YOU NEED AT 25 IS EXPERIENCE.... YOUR WHOLE LIFE IS STILL AHEAD OF YOU!!

...I WISH I WAS YOUNGER.

HERE COMES ELIZABETH'S BUS—IT'S RIGHT ON TIME.
I CAN SEE HER IN THE WINDOW!

ELIZABETH! ELIZABETH! I'VE MISSED YOU SO MUCH!
COME HERE, KIDDO! GIMME A HUG!

SO! MY TWO GIRLS ARE HAPPY TO BE TOGETHER AGAIN!

DON'T WORRY, POP... IT'LL WEAR OFF!

DUMP!

WELCOME HOME, HONEY! SUPPER'S ALMOST READY!

AWESOME, MOM!

YOU WON'T BELIEVE HOW MUCH I'VE LOOKED FORWARD TO YOUR HOME COOKING!!!

SIT UP STRAIGHT, APRIL. CHEW WITH YOUR MOUTH CLOSED.

USE YOUR KNIFE PROPERLY. CUT YOUR MEAT INTO SMALLER PIECES, AND DON'T TALK WITH YOUR MOUTH FULL.

EAT ANOTHER PIECE OF BROCCOLI, PLEASE, AND FINISH YOUR MILK. DON'T WIPE YOUR HANDS ON YOUR SHIRT, USE A NAPKIN.

THIS ISN'T BAD, MOM!

YES, IT'S HARD TO TELL THE DIFFERENCE NOW BETWEEN BOUGHT AND HOME-COOKED MEALS!

YEAH... THEY BOTH COME WITH INSTRUCTIONS.

APRIL SAYS YOU MIGHT BE MOVING SOON, GRANDPA!

IT LOOKS THAT WAY, ELIZABETH.

I PUT MY NAME ON A WAITING LIST FOR AN APARTMENT IN THE SAME BUILDING AS MY FRIEND, IRIS—AND, THERE'S AN OPENING NEXT MONTH!

WE'LL BE ON DIFFERENT FLOORS— BUT, I'LL BE RIGHT NEXT TO THE ELEVATOR.

WHY DON'T YOU JUST GET MARRIED?

NAH...

....TOO MANY UPS AND DOWNS.

71

IRIS AND I TALKED ABOUT GETTING MARRIED, LIZ.... BUT, IT WOULD BE COMPLICATED.

WHY?

OH, SHE HAS HER WAY OF DOING THINGS AND I HAVE MINE.

BESIDES, LIVING SEPARATELY IS MORE ROMANTIC. IT KEEPS THE MYSTERY IN OUR RELATIONSHIP!

....I NEVER SEE HER PLUCKING HER CHIN HAIRS AND SHE NEVER SEES ME WITHOUT MY TEETH.

ELIZABETH, WHERE ARE YOU GOING?

DAWN IS IN TOWN... WE'RE GONNA GO TO A BAR OR SOMETHING.

DRESSED LIKE THAT? —I CAN SEE YOUR NAVEL!

DAD, THIS IS TOTALLY IN FASHION! THESE CLOTHES — ARE TAME COMPARED TO WHAT SOME GIRLS WEAR!

I DON'T CARE. I STILL DISAPPROVE..

TSK

YOU ARE SO OLD FASHIONED !!!

WHAT WERE YOU TWO ARGUING ABOUT?

...THE GENERATION GAP!

THIS IS MY APARTMENT. IT WILL BE AVAILABLE IN 2 WEEKS.

THANK YOU FOR LETTING US SEE IT, SUSAN.

MY DAUGHTER WANTS ME TO MOVE TO A FACILITY NEAR HER HOME. ONE WITH 24 HOUR NURSING CARE.

WINTER CLOTHES

PHOTOS

BOOTS & SHOES

I'VE FOUGHT THE IDEA FOR LONG ENOUGH

I'M SURE YOU HATE TO GIVE UP YOUR PLACE.

I'M NOT GIVING UP MY APARTMENT, JIM. I'M GIVING UP MY INDEPENDENCE.

WHATCHA MAKIN', APRIL?

I DUNNO.....IT'S SORT OF AN EXPERIMENT.

I CALL IT A DOGWOOD SANDWICH

YOU MEAN "DAGWOOD."

A SANDWICH LIKE THAT IS CALLED A "DAGWOOD"!

NO, ELIZABETH, IT'S A DOGWOOD!!

SPLUTT

SPLOOT SPLAPP

'CAUSE I'M NOT SURE HOW IT'S GONNA TASTE

SPLORB

SO, IF I WON'T EAT IT.....

THE DOG WOULD!

THIS IS MY APARTMENT. IT WILL BE AVAILABLE IN 2 WEEKS.

THANK YOU FOR LETTING US SEE IT, SUSAN.

MY DAUGHTER WANTS ME TO MOVE TO A FACILITY NEAR HER HOME. ONE WITH 24 HOUR NURSING CARE.

I'VE FOUGHT THE IDEA FOR LONG ENOUGH

I'M SURE YOU HATE TO GIVE UP YOUR PLACE.

I'M NOT GIVING UP MY APARTMENT, JIM. I'M GIVING UP MY INDEPENDENCE.

MY SON-IN-LAW IS GOING TO MOVE ME.

THE PROBLEM WITH NURSING HOMES IS SPACE. I'LL HAVE A SMALL ROOM AND A SHARED COMMODE.

THIS IS WHAT I'M TAKING. MOSTLY PHOTO-GRAPHS, A FAVORITE CHAIR, A READING LAMP...

I WON'T MISS THE ORNAMENTS OR THE FURNITURE.

BUT, YOU HAVE SOME REAL TREASURES HERE!

PEOPLE ARE MY TREASURES, NOW. THESE ARE JUST ..."THINGS".

I'LL GIVE YOU SOME ADVICE, JIM. THE THINGS YOU'VE COLLECTED OVER THE YEARS SHOULD GO TO THE PEOPLE WHO DESERVE OR WILL APPRECIATE THEM MOST.

CALL YOUR FAMILY TOGETHER AND HAVE THEM CHOOSE THEIR FAVORITE PIECES. THEN, PUT THEIR NAMES ON THE BACK SO EVERYONE KNOWS WHAT BELONGS TO WHOM!

I'VE MADE THAT SUGGEST-ION, BUT EVERYONE KEEPS PUTTING IT OFF. MY GRAND DAUGHTER SAYS IT'S TOO "SPOOKY"!

TYPICAL!

THEY'D ALL RATHER WAIT AND FIGHT OVER STUFF WHEN WE'RE DEAD!

YOU'LL LIKE LIVING HERE, JIM. IT'S DESIGNED FOR SENIORS-THERE'S A GYM, A DINING ROOM AND MOVIE NIGHT'S ON THURSDAY!

GROCERIES CAN BE DELIVERED, AND...,

I CAN WALK MY DOG IN THE GARDEN!

DIDN'T THEY TELL YOU? THERE'S A "NO NEW PETS" POLICY! EVERYONE WHO OWNS A PET NOW CAN KEEP THEM, BUT THERE WILL BE NO NEW PETS ALLOWED IN THE BUILDING.

WHAT? I CAN'T MOVE WITHOUT DIXIE!

IT'S A RECENT EDICT. PERHAPS THEY'LL MAKE AN EXCEPTION

WHO'S "THEY"? HOW CAN I GET AN INTERVIEW WITH THESE PEOPLE?!!

...DON'T MAKE YOUR RENT PAYMENTS.

I COULD KEEP DIXIE AT MY PLACE 'TIL YOU MOVE IN, JIM!

I DON'T WANT YOU TO GET INTO TROUBLE!

I HAVEN'T SEEN THE SUPERINTENDANT OR THE MAINTANANCE MAN FOR AGES. THEY WOULDN'T KNOW I DIDN'T HAVE A DOG.

WHAT ARE YOU SUGGESTING, IRIS?

AS LONG AS DOMINIC, THE DOORMAN DOESN'T SEE US, WE COULD SNEAK HER IN!!

BUT, HOW?

I DON'T KNOW, BUT I THINK WE'RE ON A ROLL!

WHERE ARE YOU TAKING DIXIE, GRAMPA?

WHY?

TO IRIS' APARTMENT

THEY'VE JUST PASSED A NEW BYLAW, PROHIBITING ANY NEW PETS IN THE BUILDING, SO WE'RE SNEAKING HER IN, 'TIL I GET MY APARTMENT!

OH.

WE'RE HERE, DRIVER. COULD YOU WAIT FOR A MINUTE WHILE I GET A WHEELCHAIR FOR MY FRIEND?

SURE

UP GIRL!

COME ON, DIXIE!

I FEEL LIKE E.T.

SHUT UP AND LOOK FEEBLE.

GOOD EVENING, MA'AM— CAN I GIVE YOU A HAND?

NO THANK YOU, DOMINIC WE'LL BE FINE.

I THINK I SHOULD COME WITH YOU!

REALLY, MY FRIEND AND I CAN MANAGE ON OUR OWN.

BUT THERE'S A PROBLEM.

WHAT PROBLEM?

HE'S LEAKING KIBBLE.

DOMINIC, THIS IS JIM RICHARDS. HE'S MOVING INTO THE BUILDING NEXT WEEK. I WAS GOING TO KEEP HIS DOG FOR HIM UNTIL....

THERE'S AN ORDINANCE NOW THAT STATES ONLY THE PETS ALREADY HERE CAN STAY IN THE BUILDING.

BUT...

I DON'T MAKE THE RULES, MA'AM.

HAS A CENSUS BEEN TAKEN? HAS THE NEW "LAW" BEEN ACCEPTED BY THE TENANTS' ASSOCIATION? WHEN DOES THE LAW COME INTO EFFECT?

REMEMBER? YOU HAVE THE ADVANTAGE IF YOU CAN CONFUSE THE ENEMY!

WHAT'S THE MATTER, DAD?

I DON'T KNOW IF I'LL BE ABLE TO TAKE DIXIE WHEN I MOVE INTO MY NEW APARTMENT.

THE MANAGEMENT HAS DECIDED NOT TO ACCEPT ANY NEW PETS.

I DON'T REMEMBER ANY REFERRAL TO THAT ON THE PAPERS YOU SIGNED!

WELL, THEY'VE MADE AN AMENDMENT—AND THAT MEANS I PROBABLY DON'T HAVE A LEG TO STAND ON.

...I'D SAY YOU HAVE SIX!

I DON'T WANT TWO DOGS, JOHN. WHEN MY DAD MOVES, I WANT DIXIE TO GO TOO!

WITH BOTH OF US WORKING, APRIL GOING TO CAMP AND ELIZABETH WITH HER OWN PLANS.... ONE DOG AND ONE RABBIT WILL BE ENOUGH!

YOU'RE RIGHT, EL.... ONE DOG IS ENOUGH.

...WHO'S GOING TO BREAK THE NEWS TO THEM?!

Z

YOU'RE WASHING DAD'S CAR, LIZ?

YEAH! IT'S GOOD EXERCISE, AN' HE'S PAYING MY IN-SURANCE OVER THE SUMMER-SO, I OWE HIM ONE.

OK

BUT, HOW COME YOU PARKED IT AT THE VERY END OF THE DRIVEWAY?

OH.

THAT IS, LIKE A 1964 BUSHWHACKER 4X!

1962! SWEET

CAN WE TAKE A LOOK?

SURE WHOOOOO°

SO COOL!

HI, APRIL-WHERE ARE YOU OFF TO?

DOWN TO THE END OF THE DRIVEWAY TO WASH MY BIKE!

WHAT ARE YOU LOOKING FOR, EL?

I HAVE A WHOLE LOT OF PLASTIC CONTAINERS— AND, NO LIDS!

FOR SOME REASON,...THEY KEEP DISAPPEARING!

SNARP!

DAD, I CALLED THE TENNANTS' ASSOCIATION AND THE OWNER OF YOUR BUILDING.

BECAUSE YOU SIGNED THE AGREEMENT BEFORE THE NEW "NO PETS" REGULATION, YOU CAN KEEP DIXIE!

THAT'S GREAT!

I THOUGHT I WAS GOING TO HAVE TO LEAVE HER BEHIND!

NOPE!

...LOOKS LIKE YOU CAN KEEP BOTH ENDS!

YOU REALLY ARE MOVING, AREN'T YOU.

I WON'T BE TOO FAR AWAY—AND YOU CAN ALWAYS VISIT ME!

IT WON'T BE THE SAME WITHOUT GRAMPA.

NOTHING STAYS THE SAME, APRIL. THAT'S WHAT MAKES LIFE SO INTERESTING.

CHANGE OPENS DOORS! IT MAKES YOU FLEXIBLE. IT MAKES YOU STRONG.

HAVING SAID THAT, ELLY....

WOULD YOU MIND GIVING US A HAND WITH THIS DESK?

IT WAS NICE OF GORDON TO LEND US THIS TRUCK!

HE'S A FINE YOUNG MAN.

MICHAEL'S MEETING US AT YOUR APARTMENT TO HELP US UNLOAD.

IT WILL BE STRANGE, LIVING ON MY OWN AGAIN

BUT, I'M SO LOOKING FORWARD TO IT!

WHO WOULD HAVE THOUGHT THAT AT THE END OF MY LIFE, THERE'D BE A WHOLE NEW BEGINNING!

WELL, WE GOT DAD AND DIXIE SAFELY MOVED TO THEIR NEW APARTMENT.

IT'S A NICE PLACE!

THERE'S A GARDEN HE'LL ENJOY AND A PARK DOWN THE STREET. HE'LL SEE IRIS EVERY DAY....

I'M GONNA MISS HIM.

IT'LL BE DIFFERENT, ALL RIGHT.... WITH ONE LESS PERSON AND ONE LESS PET.

BUT, IN A FEW DAYS, WE'LL ALL BE BACK TO NORMAL.

?

WHAT'S THE MATTER, ED?

.....HE KEEPS LOOKING FOR DIXIE.

SHE'S NOT HERE, BOY. SHE'S GONE TO LIVE WITH GRANDPA. LIE DOWN, OK? GO TO SLEEP.

EDGAR

I PUT ONE OF HER BLANKETS NEXT TO HIS BED, BUT IT'S NOT HELPING.

HE'S USED TO SLEEPING NEXT TO HER WHAT SHOULD WE DO?

82

MICHAEL! COME AND SEE WHAT I BOUGHT FROM ONE OF THE GIRLS AT WORK!

A CRIB AND CHANGE TABLE, WIND UP SWING, FOLDING STROLLER—AND A WHOLE BOX OF CLOTHES!

SHE ONLY WANTS $50.00 FOR EVERYTHING!—DO WE HAVE THE CASH?

NO.

...HERE'S A REALITY CHECK!

HOW DID YOU GET ALL THAT BABY FURNITURE HERE, DEANNA?

MY FRIEND, CHARLOTTE FROM WORK? HER HUSBAND BROUGHT IT FOR US!

I WAS SO EXCITED, I CALLED MRS. SALTZMAN. SHE SAID EVERYTHING LOOKED SAFE AND IN GOOD CONDITION.

AND, GUESS WHAT! IF A 2 BEDROOM APARTMENT COMES UP, SHE'LL LET US HAVE IT FOR JUST $100.00 A MONTH MORE! WE COULD DO IT, MICHAEL! EVEN IF YOU WERE THE ONLY BREADWINNER!

BUT...WE'RE ALREADY LIVING ON CRUMBS!

I'M GLAD YOU CAME OVER, MIKE. IT'S BEEN A WHILE SINCE WE TALKED.

I NEED SOME ADVICE GORDO.

I LOVE MY WIFE, I'M HAPPY ABOUT THE BABY AND I'VE GOT A GOOD JOB ...BUT I'M STARTING TO RESENT EVERYTHING.

I KNOW WHAT YOU MEAN.

WHEN TRACEY WAS FIRST PREGNANT, I FELT THE WEIGHT OF THE WORLD WAS SUDDENLY ON MY SHOULDERS.

WHAT DID YOU DO?

...MADE SURE MY FEET WERE ON SOLID GROUND.

YOUR FINANCES LOOK OK, MIKE. DEE WILL HAVE SOME MONEY COMING IN — AND, YOU'RE KEEPING YOUR EXPENSES DOWN.

SHE WANTS TO GO BACK TO WORK A YEAR AFTER THE BABY'S BORN. I WAS HOPING WE'D BE ABLE TO SAVE FOR A HOUSE, BUT THAT'S A LONG WAY OFF, NOW.

YOU ARE DOING SO WELL, GORD. YOU HAVE A SUCCESSFUL BUSINESS, AND A HOME. — CONGRATULATIONS, MAN!

SOME OF US USED TO WONDER WHAT YOU WERE GONNA DO WITHOUT A UNIVERSITY EDUCATION.

AND, WHILE WE WERE IN SCHOOL, YOU WENT AHEAD AND **DID** IT!!!!

MICHAEL'S WORRIED ABOUT HOW WE'RE GOING TO SURVIVE, TRACEY.

YOU'LL BE FINE, DEE.

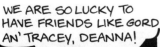

LIFE'S MORE COMPLICATED WHEN YOU HAVE KIDS — BUT, YOU'LL BE SURPRISED BY HOW QUICKLY YOU ADJUST!

I'VE READ EVERYTHING I CAN FIND — BUT, I STILL FEEL STUPID. I KNOW NOTHING ABOUT BEING A MOTHER!

NEITHER DID I!

SO, HOW DID YOU FIND OUT?

SMILE AND ERROR!

WE ARE SO LUCKY TO HAVE FRIENDS LIKE GORD AN' TRACEY, DEANNA!

I KNOW. WE'RE JUST STARTING A FAMILY, AND THEY'VE ALREADY GONE THROUGH EVERYTHING!

TWICE!

IT'S LIKE — IF THEY CAN DO IT, **WE** CAN DO IT! — VISITING THEM GIVES YOU A REAL SENSE OF CONFIDENCE!

EVEN IF WE **DON'T** KNOW WHAT WE'RE IN FOR!

REMEMBER WHEN A "NIGHT ON THE TOWN" MEANT EATING AT A PUB AND DANCING?!

DIXIE! COME BACK! DIXIE!!!

THIS NEIGHBORHOOD IS SO NEW TO HER— SHE WON'T KNOW WHERE SHE'S GOING!

DIXIE? DIXIE!!! WHAT'LL I DO IF SHE'S....

LOST?!!

MAPLE RIDGE, MAPLE GROVE, MAPLE LANE... I KNOW MY STREET CROSSES A MAPLE "SOMETHING"

DIXIE? DIXIE!

I DON'T REMEMBER THAT HOUSE! DO I GO LEFT OR RIGHT HERE? WHERE DOES THIS STREET GO?

DIXIE!!

I DON'T KNOW WHO'S MORE LOST... MY DOG OR ME!

IT'S LATE, AND IT'S COLD OUTSIDE. I JUST HAVE A LIGHT JACKET ON.

I HAVE NO IDEA WHERE I AM. I DON'T WANT TO KNOCK ON A STRANGER'S DOOR....

I SHOULDN'T BE SO AFRAID. I'VE ONLY BEEN WALKING FOR A SHORT WHILE. MY APARTMENT SHOULD BE VERY NEAR HERE.

WHERE ARE THE POLICE WHEN YOU NEED THEM?!

 WHHHHTTT

 WHHHFFFTTT

 APRIL, HONEY... LET ME CUT YOUR HAIR SO IT WON'T FALL INTO YOUR EYES!

 NOOO, MOM! BUT, YOU CAN'T SEE!

 I LIKE IT LIKE THIS.

 WHHHTTT!

 WE COULD GO TO A NICE SALON AND HAVE A PROFESSIONAL DO IT! NAH.

 BUT, IT LOOKS SO UNTIDY DOESN'T BOTHER ME!

 HEY! APRIL!!

 WHAT'S WITH THE HAIR OVER YOUR FACE?! YEAH! YOU'RE NOT **THAT** UGLY! BEAR CLAW

 SNIP SNIP SNIP!

I LOVE MY DOG, IRIS.... BUT I DON'T KNOW HOW SENSIBLE IT IS TO KEEP HER IN THIS APARTMENT.

SHE HAS NO PLACE TO RUN, SHE HATES THE ELEVATOR, I DON'T WALK HER AS OFTEN AS I SHOULD ...IT REALLY ISN'T FAIR.

WHAT AM I GOING TO DO? I HATE TO LET HER GO. ..... SHE'S BEEN A GOOD PET, AND A WONDERFUL COMPANION

WOULD YOU BE HAPPY WITH AN OLD BIRD LIKE ME?

HEY, MOM! IT'S GRAMPA! HE WANTS TO KNOW IF WE'LL TAKE DIXIE BACK!

HE SAYS IT'S HARD TO WALK HER, AN HE EVEN GOT LOST THE OTHER NIGHT 'CAUSE SHE RAN AWAY.

I SAID IT WOULD BE TOTALLY COOL TO HAVE HER BACK 'CAUSE EDDY MISSES HER SO MUCH. IS THAT OK?

:SIGH: THESE DAYS, FAMILY DECISIONS ARE OFTEN BASED ON WHO'S FIRST TO ANSWER THE PHONE.

I'M SO GLAD YOU'LL TAKE DIXIE, ELLY. I KNOW YOU DIDN'T WANT TWO DOGS!

BUT, SHE'S SO AT HOME HERE. SHE MISSED EDDY AND THE KIDS AND THE FREEDOM...

IT'S OK, DAD... I HALF EXPECTED THIS TO HAPPEN.

...AND THE OTHER HALF HOPED IT WOULDN'T.

DUNCAN! WHAT'S UP?

MY DAD WAS COMIN' OVER TO CHECK OUT YOUR DAD'S TRAINS...

SO, I CAME ALONG TO SEE IF YOU WANTED TO DO SOMETHING.

SURE!

WHAT DO YOU WANNA DO?

I DUNNO... WHAT DO YOU WANNA DO?

EASY ON THAT SWITCH DEAN. OK, LET'S ATTACH THOSE ORE CARS.

LIZ-IF YOU'RE JUST HANGING AROUND, COULD YOU BRING US A COLD BEER?

UH... SURE.

"HANGING AROUND" THAT REALLY BURNS MY BUTT! AS IF I WAS STANDING AROUND, DOING ABSOLUTELY **NOTHING**!!

HERE, DAD.

THANKS, HON.

WHATCHA DOING, LIZ?

WAITING FOR A FRIEND.

A FRIEND? LIKE A GUY FRIEND?!

JUST A FRIEND, OK? NOTHING SPECIAL. JUST SOMEONE I KNOW FROM WORK.

SO, IT'S A "NOTHING-BETTER-TO-DO" KIND OF DATE!!!

APRIL, WOULD YOU GO JUMP OFF A CLIFF OR SOMETHING?!!

YOU CAN REALLY BUG ME SOMETIMES!!

IT'S NICE TO KNOW I HAVEN'T LOST MY TOUCH!

WHAT'S WITH YOUR SISTER?

OH, SHE ALWAYS ACTS WEIRD WHEN SHE'S WAITING FOR A DATE.

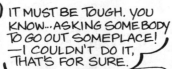

IT MUST BE TOUGH. YOU KNOW... ASKING SOMEBODY TO GO OUT SOMEPLACE! —I COULDN'T DO IT, THAT'S FOR SURE.

ME NEITHER.

I MEAN, IF THEY SAID "NO" IT WOULD BE, LIKE, MAJOR EMBARRASSMENT! TOTAL MENTAL MELTDOWN!

REALLY.

WANNA GO TO THE CORNER STORE FOR A POP?

SURE, WHY NOT.

DAD, DUNCAN AN' I WANNA GO TO THE CORNER STORE. COULD WE HAVE SOME, UH....

MONEY?

SURE! IF YOU TWO SWEEP OUT THE GARAGE, FOLD THE BOXES FOR RECYCLING AND BRUSH THE DOGS...

I'LL GIVE YOU 5 BUCKS

EACH?!!

TOTAL.

OH.

I'LL MAKE IT MORE IF YOU DO A REALLY, REALLY, REALLY GOOD JOB!

WHAT DO YOU THINK, DUNCAN?

WE'LL TAKE THE 5.

SEE YOU LATER, DAD.

HAVE FUN, HONEY.

I'M GLAD MY KIDS AREN'T OLD ENOUGH TO BE DATING!

IT'S TOUGH, DEAN!

YOU HAVE TO LET THEM GO... AND, EVENTUALLY, YOU SEE THAT ALL THE WORRY, CONFRONTATIONS AND DISCIPLINE HAVE PAID OFF.

YOU HAVE TWO ADULT CHILDREN, JOHN. HOW LONG DOES IT TAKE?

...WE'RE NOT SURE YET.

IT WAS MY LAST DAY AT WORK TODAY, MICHAEL. THE GIRLS GAVE ME A SURPRISE SHOWER!

LITTLE SLIPPERS, COTTON SLEEPERS, OVERALLS...

THEY'RE ALL SO... TINY!

I CAN REALLY FEEL YOUR TUMMY MOVE!

AMAZING, ISN'T IT!

I WONDER IF OUR BABY IS THINKING ANYTHING RIGHT NOW!

?!!

SO, WE PLAN TO MOVE OUR BED, FIT THE CRIB IN HERE AND THE CHANGE TABLE WILL GO IN THE HALL!

HMM.

I'VE BEEN THINKING. IF YOU FIXED UP THIS PORCH, IT COULD BE LIKE A SMALL BEDROOM!

...A LITTLE PAINT, A LITTLE CARPET, BETTER WINDOWS...

LOVEY, THAT'S A GREAT IDEA!

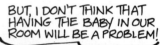

BUT, I DON'T THINK THAT HAVING THE BABY IN OUR ROOM WILL BE A PROBLEM!

THAT'S BECAUSE IT'S QUIET NOW!

LISTEN. WE'LL HELP WITH THE PORCH. A NEW WINDOW, I'LL PAY FOR AND ALSO THE DOOR. IT NEEDS DOING ANYWAY.

A LITTLE HEAT, SOME PICTURES, CURTAINS - AND YOU'VE GOT A SPARE ROOM!

A SPARE ROOM!

BEING CLOSE TO YOUR SMALL CHILDREN IS A GOOD THING, DEANNA!

BUT, EQUALLY GOOD IS GETTING AWAY FROM THEM!

MOM! WHAT A SURPRISE! —I WANT YOU TO MEET OUR LANDLADY, LOVEY SALTZMAN.

A PLEASURE.

SHE'S GOING TO HELP ME CONVERT OUR BACK PORCH INTO A BABY'S ROOM!

A PORCH, DEANNA?

WE'LL FIX THE WINDOW, GET SOME PAINT... IT'LL BE PERFECT!

AND, THIS CRIB AND STROLLER?

I BOUGHT THEM FROM A FRIEND FOR 50 DOLLARS!

WELL... I'M SURE YOU CAN GET RID OF THEM

WE DON'T WANT OUR BRAND NEW BABY USING SECOND HAND THINGS!

DEANNA, I'VE BOUGHT YOU AN ENTIRE BEDROOM ENSEMBLE FOR THE LITTLE ONE!

BUT....

WITH MATCHING CHANGE TABLE, LINENS AND TOYS.

MOM, I'M SO HAPPY WITH WHAT WE HAVE!

YOUR FATHER AND I WOULD LIKE YOU TO MOVE TO A BIGGER APARTMENT. WE'VE MADE SOME ENQUIRIES, AND FOUND SOMETHING NICE.

YOU DID?!

DON'T YOU THINK YOU SHOULD HAVE TALKED ALL THIS OVER WITH US FIRST?!!!

WHAT?....

...AND RUIN THE SURPRISE?!

MOM, I TRULY APPRECIATE YOUR THOUGHTFULNESS, BUT...

DON'T RAISE YOUR VOICE, DEAR. IT STARTLES THE BABY.

LOOK, THIS IS NOT MY BUSINESS, MRS. SOBINSKI— BUT WE SHOULD TALK.

ABOUT WHAT?

COME. WE'RE BOTH GRANDMOTHERS, WE'VE SEEN DIFFICULT TIMES, WE SHARE THE SAME SENTIMENTS...

I TOO WANTED THE BEST FOR MY DAUGHTER. EVERY DAY, I GAVE HER ADVICE. I SAID: "CYNTHIA, YOU SHOULD DO WHAT'S BEST FOR YOUR FAMILY!"

AND?...

....THEY ALL PACKED UP AND MOVED TO SEATTLE.

DAD...HOW CAN YOU TELL IF A GUY IS HONEST AND DECENT AND NICE?

EVERYONE SEEMS TOTALLY GREAT WHEN YOU FIRST MEET THEM....

SO, YOU GET INVOLVED—....AND **THEN**, YOU FIND OUT THEY'RE SOME KIND OF DIRT-BALL!!!

THAT'S A TOUGH QUESTION, LIZ....BUT I HAVE A THEORY:

YOU CAN TELL A LOT ABOUT A MAN BY THE WAY HE TREATS HIS VEHICLE!

SOMEONE WHO LET'S HIS CAR RUST OUT, AND WAITS FOR THE ENGINE TO SEIZE PROBABLY HAS THE SAME DIS- REGARD FOR THE PEOPLE HE HANGS OUT WITH.

BEEP! BEEP!

S'CUSE ME, POP—I GOT A DATE.

MIRA SOBINSKI:—YOU'RE POLISH!

ME TOO.

YES.

MY PARENTS CAME TO CANADA AS REFUGEES IN THE 40'S

MINE, TOO.

THEY HAD ABSOLUTELY NOTHING. BUT MY FATHER BUILT A SMALL BUSINESS AND MADE MONEY ENOUGH TO BUY US A HOUSE, PUT FOOD ON THE TABLE AND SEND US TO SCHOOL.

MINE, TOO.

MY PARENTS SACRIFICED TO GIVE ME EVERYTHING!

YOU HAVE **EVERYTHING?**

MY TWO SISTERS AND I WENT TO UNIVERSITY. I WAS A TEACHER FOR THIRTY YEARS.

MY HUSBAND'S PARENTS SACRIFICED FOR HIM, AND HE DID WELL. WE HAVE TWO NICE CHILDREN—A BOY, 36 AND A DAUGHTER, 32.

WE OWN TWO HOUSES AND, IN TORONTO, THAT'S GOOD! MORRIE AND I ARE HEALTHY. TO ME, WE HAVE EVERYTHING!

WELL...WHEN YOU LOOK AT IT THAT WAY—I GUESS WE HAVE EVERYTHING, TOO!

BUT...I WANT MORE.

I TALK TO YOUR DAUGHTER OFTEN. SHE'S A SWEET GIRL.

THANK YOU, MRS.....

CALL ME "LOVEY"

SHE SHOWED ME THE GIFTS YOU'VE GIVEN HER—MIRA, ONE BABY CAN'T USE SO MUCH!

WHAT?

LOOK, IT'S NONE OF MY BUSINESS, BUT YOUNG PEOPLE SHOULDN'T HAVE THINGS HANDED TO THEM. LIFE SHOULDN'T BE EASY!

WHAT, YOU THINK PEOPLE SHOULD SUFFER?!

YES. THEY SHOULD SUFFER! YOU GROW WHEN YOU SUFFER! YOU LEARN WHEN YOU SUFFER! EVERYONE SHOULD SUFFER!

...BUT, NOT TOO MUCH.

MY DAUGHTER'S LANDLADY IS TELLING ME HOW TO RAISE MY CHILD!

SHE'S RAISED-AND YOU DID A GOOD JOB!

NOW, SEE HOW WELL SHE CAN DO ON HER OWN! LET HER BUY SECOND HAND! LET HER DO THINGS HER WAY!

THIS FROM A WOMAN WHO ADMITS HER DAUGHTER MOVED TO SEATTLE, TO GET **AWAY** FROM HER?

I'VE MADE MISTAKES. YES.

SO, WHY SHOULD I TAKE ADVICE FROM YOU?

BECAUSE....MISTAKES ARE WHERE ADVICE COMES FROM!

YOUR MOM'S CAR IS OUTSIDE...WHERE IS SHE?

NEXT DOOR, HAVING A DRINK WITH LOVEY.

WHAT DID SHE BRING THIS TIME?

BABY CLOTHES....BUT SHE'S ORDERED A NEW CRIB AND A LOT OF OTHER THINGS.

BUT, WE ALREADY HAVE A CRIB, A STROLLER, A CAR SEAT...

MOM WANTS THE BABY TO HAVE EVERY- THING NEW!

THAT'S CRAZY! THE STUFF WE HAVE IS PERFECTLY GOOD —AND A BABY DOESN'T CARE WHAT HE SLEEPS IN!

I KNOW...

BUT I WANT MY **MOM** TO BE COMFORTABLE!

IT WOULD BE NICE TO HAVE NEW BABY FURNITURE, MICHAEL. WE COULD SELL WHAT WE HAVE AND KEEP THE THINGS MY MOM BOUGHT!

BUT, YOU WERE SO HAPPY WITH.....

I KNOW-IT'S JUST THAT NEW STUFF WOULD BE IN- CREDIBLE! -AND IT WOULD BE **FREE!**

HELLO, YOU TWO! I'VE JUST HAD A GREAT CHAT WITH YOUR LANDLADY!

MOM, WE WANT TO TALK TO YOU ABOUT THE THINGS YOU ORDERED.

I KNOW...

AND DON'T WORRY... I'VE DECIDED TO SEND IT ALL BACK!

CLANG CLANG CLANG

OH, NO!!

WE'RE ALREADY LATE!

FOUR ENGINES! THIS IS GOING TO BE A LONG TRAIN!

4370

LOOK AT ALL THE CARS, JOHN. WE'LL BE STOPPED HERE FOR AGES!

THIS IS SO FRUSTRATING!

I KNOW.

...WE'D BE ABLE TO SEE IT SO MUCH BETTER...IF WE WERE FIRST IN LINE!

CN

DAD, COULD I TRADE CARS WITH YOU TODAY?

YOU WANT ME TO DRIVE YOUR BLUE "JUNKER"?

PLEASE? I WANNA PICK UP SOME FRIENDS AN' GO DOWN TO THE BEACH AFTER WORK.

PLEASE? YOU KNOW I'LL TAKE CARE OF IT. WE'LL WASH IT FOR YOU! PLEASE, DAD? PLEEEEEASE?

THANKS!!!

IT'S HOW YOU SAY "PLEASE" THAT GETS YOU THE KEYS!!

ELIZABETH, IF YOU'RE GOING BY GORD'S GARAGE, WOULD YOU DROP IN FOR A MINUTE?

NO PROBLEM!

GET SOME GAS, CHECK THE OIL.

NO PROBLEM.

TOP UP THE WINDSHIELD FLUID...CHECK THE TIRES...

NO PROBLEM.

AND I HAVE A BANK STATEMENT HERE, YOU CAN GIVE TO ANTHONY.

PROBLEM!

HI, GORDON! DAD ASKED ME TO BRING HIS CAR OVER...

ONE OF THE BOYS WILL TAKE CARE OF IT!—COME ON IN, LIZ!

I HAVEN'T SEEN YOU FOR AGES!

THIS PLACE HAS SURE CHANGED!

WE SEEM TO BE GROWING EVERY YEAR-AND I'LL GIVE YOUR DAD MUCH OF THE CREDIT. HE'S HELPED US A LOT!

I KNOW

HE LIKES TO SAY HIS INVESTMENTS ARE IN GAS AND OIL!

HI, DAWN! SORRY I MISSED YOUR CALL. I WAS DOWNTOWN WITH MY MOM.

IT WAS SO COOL! WE WENT EVERYWHERE AN' FOR THE FIRST TIME IN AGES, I DIDN'T FEEL LIKE AN IDIOT! SHE NEVER EMBARRASSED ME ONCE! IT WAS LIKE WE WERE SISTERS!

MAN, I CAN'T BELIEVE HOW MUCH SHE'S CHANGED!

Panel 1: WHAT DO YOU HAVE HERE? / A BANK STATEMENT. DAD ASKED ME TO GIVE IT TO ANTHONY.

Panel 2: IS HE HERE? / SURE IS!—GREAT GUY. ...DON'T KNOW WHAT WE'D DO WITHOUT HIM!

Panel 3: HE'S ENGAGED NOW—TO A NICE GIRL CALLED THÉRÈSE.

Panel 4: WHICH REALLY AMAZES ME! / WHY?

Panel 5: ...I ALWAYS THOUGHT HE'D BE ENGAGED TO YOU!

Panel 6: ANTHONY? / ELIZABETH! WOW!—IS IT EVER NICE TO SEE YOU!!!

Panel 7: I HAVEN'T CALLED YOU BECAUSE... / I KNOW. I HAVEN'T CALLED YOU EITHER—"BECAUSE".

Panel 8: UM, DAD ASKED ME TO GIVE YOU THIS. IT'S FROM THE BANK. / GREAT!—HE'S PUTTING MORE MONEY INTO GORD'S BUSINESS, YOU KNOW!

Panel 9: HE CALLS IT HIS RETIREMENT PLAN.

Panel 10: YOU LOOK GREAT! HOW'S SCHOOL? WHAT'S GOING ON? TELL ME EVERYTHING! / THERE'S NOT MUCH TO TELL.

Panel 11: SCHOOL'S GOOD I'LL BE PRACTICE TEACHING THIS FALL. I THINK I'LL BE RENTING A HOUSE WITH CANDACE AND ANOTHER GIRL.

Panel 12: I'M NOT DATING ANYONE. I WAS, BUT YOU KNOW HOW IT IS.... I'M STILL PAYING FOR MY MISTAKES.

Panel 13: AND, YOU'RE ENGAGED. / UH-HUH ...I'M STILL PAYING FOR THE RING!

I WANT YOU TO MEET THÉRÈSE. SHE'S A GREAT GIRL!

WHEN ARE YOU GETTING MARRIED?

Country Kitc

I DUNNO—SOMETIME AFTER WE GRADUATE. WE'RE BOTH SO SICK OF SCHOOL! PERSONALLY, I'M READY TO QUIT NOW, BUT I WANT THAT "PIECE OF PAPER".

ISN'T IT AMAZING HOW SO MUCH OF OUR FUTURE IS DETERMINED BY A CERTAIN "PIECE OF PAPER"?

ARE YOU REFERRING TO A DIPLOMA OR A MARRIAGE LICENCE?

I'M GLAD YOU'RE HAPPY, ANTHONY.

THERE'S SOMETHING I HAVEN'T TOLD YOU, LIZ.

GORDON'S ASKED ME TO MANAGE HIS BUSINESSES!

WELL, I'M NOT SURPRISED!

NOBODY KNOWS WHAT GOES ON HERE BETTER THAN YOU!—YOU'VE BEEN DOING HIS BOOKKEEPING SINCE HIGH SCHOOL!

YEAH...

...AND, HE'S BEEN DOING EVERYTHING ELSE!

I HAVE TO GO, ANTHONY. I START WORK AT MEGA-FOOD SOON.

I GUESS I HAVE TO GET BACK TO WORK, TOO.

WE'LL HAVE TO GET TOGETHER. YOU KNOW, HAVE LUNCH. THÉRÈSE IS WORKING FOR MY DAD, SO WE COULD ARRANGE A DATE!

SURE!

I'LL CALL YOU SOMETIME!

OR, I'LL CALL YOU SOMETIME.

COOL!

ONE WAY TO SAY "GOODBYE" WITHOUT SAYING "GOODBYE" IS TO SAY "I'LL CALL YOU SOMETIME".

ELLY, THERE'S A CUSTOMER HERE WHO COLLECTS CAROUSEL ORNAMENTS, AND WE DON'T HAVE ANY

TELL HER TO CHECK "CRAFTS AND CURIOS"

EXCUSE ME. DO YOU HAVE ANY BOOKS ON QUILTING?

LOOK IN "CRAFTS AND CURIOS" DOWN THE STREET.

I'M LOOKING FOR SOMETHING "GIFTY" WITH ANGELS ON IT

TRY "CRAFTS AND CURIOS"

THANK YOU SO MUCH!

YOU'RE WELCOME.

WHAT DID SHE BUY?

NOTHING... SHE'S FROM CRAFTS AND CURIOS.

WE GOT SOME OF OUR CHRISTMAS ORDER IN... WHERE SHOULD I PUT IT?

HOW ABOUT IN THE BASEMENT WHERE IT SAYS "CHRISTMAS ORDERS"?

WHERE DO YOU WANT ME TO PUT THE TONNER FILE?

IN THE FILE DRAWER UNDER "T"

THERE'S A BOOK SALESMAN HERE. WHAT SHOULD I DO?

WELL, WE DO SELL BOOKS, KORTNEY. ASK HIM TO COME HERE TO THE OFFICE, PLEASE!

I LIKE WORKING HERE, MOIRA. I JUST WISH ELLY WOULD STOP TELLING ME WHAT TO DO.

COULD I LOOK AT THAT MODEL, PLEASE?

CERTAINLY.

AND THIS OTHER ONE?

SURE!

COULD I LOOK AT THE TRUCK AND THE MODEL "T"

OK.

WHICH ONE ARE YOU INTERESTED IN?

OH... I'M NOT GONNA BUY ANYTHING...

I JUST WANTED TO LOOK AT THEM

HI, WE'RE ASKING FOR GIFT DONATIONS FOR THE HOSPITAL VOLUNTEERS!

I HAVE A BOOK SET FOR YOU!

THIS IS THE TEDDY BEAR WE PLEDGED FOR THE CHARITY SILENT AUCTION

THANKS, MRS. PATTERSON!

OUR JUNIOR BASEBALL TEAMS NEED PRIZES FOR OUR BIG TOURNAMENT.

I LIKE THE WAY YOU SUPPORT ALL THE NON-PROFIT ORGANIZATIONS, ELLY.

YES...WE'RE ABOUT AS NON-PROFIT AS YOU GET!

THE CHRISTMAS SALES WILL PULL US OUT OF THIS SLUMP, EL. WE DID WELL LAST YEAR.

AND, WE'VE SOLD ENOUGH OF OUR SUMMER STOCK TO PAY THE BILLS.

I KNOW...

I JUST THOUGHT WE'D BE MORE SUCCESSFUL BY NOW.

ELLY- THIS IS RETAIL!

THIS **IS** SUCCESS!!!

YOU TOOK OVER THIS SHOP BECAUSE YOU WANTED TO MAKE IT INTO SOMETHING MORE DIVERSE AND EXCITING.

AND, YOU DID IT! NO OTHER SHOP CARRIES THE KINDS OF THINGS WE DO OR IS AS MUCH FUN TO WORK IN!

IT ISN'T MAKING A FORTUNE, BUT IT'S SURE MADE US HAPPY!

YOU'RE RIGHT, MOIRA. IT'S SURE MADE US HAPPY.

WHY ARE YOU TWO HUGGING? .... DID SOMEBODY **BUY** SOMETHING?

SIGH

COME ON, DOGS... LET'S GO FOR A WALK.

HEY, EL!—WANT A PIECE OF CHEESECAKE?

NO, THANKS.

I'M DESPERATE TO LOSE SOME WEIGHT!

AND, I SAY TO YOU—POLLUTION IS NOT GOING TO GO AWAY! IRRESPONSIBLE DISPOSAL OF UNTREATED WASTE IS NOT GOING TO STOP! DO NOT KID YOURSELVES MY FRIENDS!

THE RESULT? GLOBAL WARMING! THE LEGACY OF OUR CAPITALIST GREEDMONGERS! THIS GENERATION WILL FRY ON EARTH BEFORE THEY FRY IN HADES!

THUS, GLOBAL WAR IS IMINENT! NOBODY PROSPERS FROM PEACE! SO, PREPARE YOURSELVES FOR THE COMING OF **DOOM!** LIFE AS WE KNOW IT WILL CEASE TO EXIST!!!! PREPARE! PREPARE!!

TWO DOUBLE X SCOOPS, PLEASE. WHITE CHOCOLATE PISTACHIO AND MAPLE WALNUT.

25 FLAVORS

"APRIL, YOUR PARENTS ARE HERE!"

"YEAH?"

"YESSS! CAN'T WAIT! OH YEAH! YA-HOOOO..."

"SWEET! THIS IS SO COOL. I AM PUMPED, MAN, I AM SO EXCITED!"

"WAIT, MOM, NO!.... PLEASE DON'T HUG ME IN PUBLIC!"

"I'M REALLY GLAD YOU GUYS ARE HERE!"

"WE COULDN'T MISS THE BIG GRANDE FINALE!"

"WE HAVE HAD AN AMAZING TIME AT MUSIC CAMP—AN' YOU WILL NOT BELIEVE THE PERFORMANCE WE'RE GONNA PUT ON TONIGHT!"

"WE GET TO SHOW YOU WHAT WE CAN DO! EVERY-KID HAS BEEN PRACTICING LIKE **CRAZY**!!!"

"EVEN THE ONES WHOSE PARENTS DON'T COME!"

"THAT'S CENTRE HALL WHERE THE SHOW WILL BE. GIRLS' CABINS ARE RIGHT, BOYS LEFT. WE'VE GOT A DINING ROOM WHICH IS ALSO FOR CRAFTS AN' 4 PRACTICE ROOMS WITH RECORDING STUFF!"

"AN' I GOTTA TELL YOU... ONE OF THE TEACHERS IS SO **HOT**!!!"

"APRIL!"

"YOU ARE TOO YOUNG TO BE SAYING THINGS LIKE THAT!"

"YEAH!"

"WHERE IS HE?"

WELCOME, FRIENDS AND FAMILIES TO OUR ORILLIA MUSIC CAMP'S "GRAND FINALE"!

WE OPEN TONIGHT WITH APRIL PATTERSON, ALVA GEROUX AND DANILO JUAREZ WITH THE BEATLES' CLASSIC "ELEANOR RIGBY"

OH, I AM SO EMOTIONAL! THIS IS ONE OF MY FAVORITE PIECES!

MOM....

THEY HAVEN'T EVEN STARTED YET!

THESE CHILDREN PERFORM SO WELL! THE MUSIC SOUNDS ALMOST PROFESSIONAL!

IT'S WONDERFUL TO SEE SUCH A CONTROLLED AND DISCIPLINED GROUP!

CLAP FWEEE CLAP CLAP CLAP WHEEP WHEEE

I'M GLAD YOU MADE SO MANY FRIENDS, APRIL!

SNIFF ... I WISH I DIDN'T HAFTA LEAVE.

DON'T WORRY, HONEY. YOU'LL BE BACK THERE BEFORE YOU KNOW IT!

WE'RE ALMOST HOME. I WANT GRANDPA TO HEAR WHAT YOU CAN PLAY ON THE GUITAR!

MY GUITAR!

I LEFT IT BACK AT MUSIC CAMP!!!

111

THIS IS A GOOD ARRANGEMENT, IRIS. ELLY BRINGS DIXIE TO ME FOR 3 DAYS A WEEK!

I CAN ENJOY MY DOG, AND DIXIE KNOWS SHE'LL BE GOING HOME TO EDDY AND THE BIG BACK YARD!

IT'S A BIT OF A NUISANCE FOR MY DAUGHTER, BUT SHE DOESN'T MIND.

YOU HAVE A GREAT FAMILY, JIM

WOULD YOU LIKE TO BE PART OF IT?

JIM, ARE YOU PROPOSING TO ME?

IRIS, WE'RE LIVING IN THE SAME BUILDING, PAYING TWO RENTS ... BUT WE SPEND ALL OUR TIME TOGETHER.

IS THIS A PROPOSAL?

WE ARE MORE THAN ..... JUST GOOD FRIENDS

ARE YOU ASKING ME TO MARRY YOU?

WELL ... I AM HOPING YOU'LL CONSIDER A LEGAL ARRANGEMENT THAT WOULD BE A SENSIBLE ALTERNATIVE TO...

I ACCEPT !!!

DAD, I'M SO HAPPY FOR YOU!

I WAS HOPING IT WOULD BE OK.

MOM WOULD HAVE WANTED YOU TO MARRY AGAIN - AND IRIS IS ALREADY PART OF THE FAMILY!

SINCE THERE ARE TWO SETS OF CHILDREN, WE'RE HAVING AN AGREEMENT DRAWN UP. WE DON'T WANT ANY BICKERING ABOUT INHERITANCE!

DAD, THAT SHOULDN'T BE A PROBLEM!

I KNOW. WITH A BIT OF LUCK, WE'LL HAVE SPENT IT ALL ANYWAY!

GRAMPA, DID I HEAR YOU SAY YOU'RE GETTING MARRIED? —WHEN?!

I'M NOT SURE... QUITE SOON, I SHOULD THINK.

BUT I'M GOING BACK TO SCHOOL THIS WEEK! I'LL MISS EVERYTHING!

DON'T WORRY, ELIZABETH.

WE HAVE TO SEND OUT INVITATIONS, PEOPLE WILL BE COMING FROM OUT OF TOWN, SO WE'LL BE ARRANGING ACCOMMODATIONS, RENTING A HALL—WE'LL HAVE TO DECORATE FOR THE CEREMONY, PLAN A RECEPTION ... A LOT WILL HAPPEN BEFORE THE WEDDING!

...I COULD DIE FIRST!!!

DO YOU NEED ANY HELP, HONEY?

NO THANKS— I'M OK.

BUT, I'LL NEED A BOX FOR STUFF I BOUGHT THIS SUMMER AN' MAYBE I'LL SWIPE ONE OF MIKE'S OLD HOCKEY BAGS.

EVERY TIME SHE LEAVES, SHE TAKES A LITTLE MORE WITH HER. SOME DAY, HER CLOSET WILL BE EMPTY, AND THIS WILL BE JUST ANOTHER SPARE ROOM.

...BUT, NOT YET.

YOU'RE HAPPY ABOUT LEAVING, AREN'T YOU, LIZ.

APRIL, I LOVE BEING HOME, OK?

BUT, I HAVE MY LIFE TO GET ON WITH! WHEN I'M HOME FOR A WHOLE SUMMER IT'S LIKE I'M A "KID" AGAIN. I HAVE NO PRIVACY.

MOM ALWAYS ASKS WHERE I'M GOING AN' WHEN I'LL BE BACK, DAD HAS TO KNOW WHO I'M WITH...

I TRY ON ALL YOUR UNDERWEAR....

YOU WHAT ?!

SHE MUST BE WEARING A "THONG".

114

'BYE, UGLY BROTHER! CALL ME WHEN THE BABY COMES!

BYE, MOM, DAD—MY RIDE IS HERE!

HAVE YOU GOT YOUR TICKET, YOUR WALLET, "KLEENEX"?

SAFE TRIP, HON.

HERE'S A BOOK, SOME SNACKS, AND EXTRA CASH. CALL WHEN YOU GET THERE.

YOU'RE WONDERFUL! THANKS FOR EVERY-THING.....I LOVE YOU!!!

WHEW! THAT WAS A FAST CONVERSATION!

AND, ALL I CAN RE-MEMBER ARE THE LAST 3 WORDS.

IT'S GOING TO COST EXTRA FOR THAT BOX, MISS. YOU'RE ALREADY OVER THE LIMIT.

I'VE ONLY GOT ONE PACK, CAN IT GO ON MY TICKET?

WHY NOT!

THANKS!

NO PROBLEM

PARCELS TAKEN AT SIDE WINDOW

SO, YOU'RE GOING UP TO NORTH BAY!

YEAH. I'M GONNA TRAIN TO FLY HELICOPTERS. I'VE ALREADY GOT MY PILOT'S LICENCE— VFR AND IFR.

11

WHAT'S VFR AND IFR?

VFR MEANS "VISUAL FLIGHT REGULATIONS", AN' IFR MEANS "I FOLLOW ROADS"

SO, YOU'RE GOING TO BE A HELICOPTER PILOT!

I'VE WANTED TO FLY SINCE I WAS A KID.

THAT'S SO COOL!

ONE TIME, WHEN I WAS 4, MY DAD SAID IF I FLAPPED MY ARMS HARD ENOUGH, I'D TAKE OFF.

SO, I RAN AROUND THE YARD—FLAPPING AND FLAPPING, AND HE KEPT YELLING "FASTER, FASTER!"

HOW DID YOU FIGURE OUT THAT HE WAS KIDDING YOU?

MY BIG BROTHER WAS ON THE GROUND LAUGH-ING, AND MOM RAN OUT WITH THE SUPER-8.

116

ELLY... WHY DON'T YOU EVER WEAR YOUR HAIR DOWN?

YOU ALWAYS HAD IT GENTLY TIED BACK OR LOOSE AROUND YOUR SHOULDERS.

I'M TOO OLD FOR THAT, NOW.

THEN, WHY DON'T YOU CUT IT?

I LIKE IT UP. IT STAYS OUT OF MY FACE.

BESIDES, I HATE THE BACK OF MY HEAD. THIS MAKES IT LOOK BETTER.

YOU **WHAT**?!!

WHAT'S WRONG WITH THE BACK OF YOUR HEAD?!

IT'S FLAT.

I'VE HATED IT SINCE I WAS A KID! .... THE BUN ROUNDS IT OUT, DON'T YOU THINK?

YOU KNOW, GORD-NO MATTER HOW LONG YOU'RE MARRIED TO YOUR WIFE, YOU'LL NEVER STOP DISCOVERING THINGS YOU DIDN'T KNOW ABOUT HER!

THANKS FOR MEETING ME, CANDACE!

SO, WHO'S THE HOTTIE?

A GUY I MET ON THE BUS. HE WANTS TO BE A HELICOPTER PILOT!

DID HE ASK FOR YOUR ADDRESS?

YES, BUT I DIDN'T GIVE IT TO HIM. HE KNOWS WHERE I'LL BE ON CAMPUS. IF HE WANTS TO SEE ME AGAIN - I'LL BE AROUND.

PLAYING HARD TO GET?

NOPE... PLAYING HARD TO HURT.

HOW WAS YOUR SUMMER, LIZ?

OK, BUT I THINK I'LL STAY UP NORTH NEXT YEAR. AFTER HAVING MY FREEDOM, IT'S SO HARD TO LIVE WITH MY FOLKS AGAIN.

FREEDOM IS GOOD, MAN- BUT THERE'S PERKS TO BEING HOME! NO RENT, NO GROCERY BILLS, NO CAR INSURANCE... YOU MUST HAVE SAVED A **WAD!**

I DID OK, BUT I SPENT A LOT MORE THAN I EXPECTED TO

ON WHAT?!!

...GETTING OUT OF THE HOUSE!

CANDACE, IS THIS THE HOUSE YOU RENTED? - IT'S FABULOUS!

THERE'S 3 BEDROOMS, TWO CANS, A WORKING FIREPLACE AN' A BEER FRIDGE ON THE PORCH!

COOL!

ANITA'S GOT THE FRONT ROOM, I'M IN THE MIDDLE, AN' WE SAVED THE BIGGEST ROOM FOR YOU.

WHY ME?

...OH.

119

Panel 1:
DEANNA, GUESS WHAT!— MY GRANDFATHER AND IRIS ELOPED! THEY'RE IN ENGLAND!!!

Panel 2:
MICHAEL, ARE YOU SERIOUS?

THEY DIDN'T WANT A PLANNED FAMILY WEDDING, SO THEY GOT MARRIED AND HOPPED A FLIGHT TO ENGLAND!

Panel 3:
AT THEIR AGE!

THEY'RE WITH A VETERAN'S TOUR GROUP. HE'S BEEN WANTING TO GO BACK AND SEE SOME OF THE PLACES HE REMEMBERED SO VIVIDLY FROM THE WAR.

Panel 4:

Panel 5:
HERE'S WHERE 408 SQUADRON WAS BASED. THERE'S NOT MUCH LEFT TO SEE NOW, BUT THE COUNTRYSIDE HASN'T CHANGED.

Panel 6:
WHEN WE WERE ON LEAVE, MARIAN AND I USED TO BICYCLE EVERYWHERE.

Panel 7:
WE MADE MANY FRIENDS HERE IN ENGLAND... AND LOST SOME, TOO. THIS BRINGS BACK SO MANY MEMORIES.

Panel 8:
MAYBE YOU WOULD RATHER COME HERE ALONE!

OH, NO. THIS IS ALL PART OF MY PAST.

Panel 9:
AND, IRIS... YOU ARE ALL OF MY FUTURE.

Panel 10:
THAT'S RIGHT, CONNIE. MY DAD MARRIED HIS FRIEND IRIS IN SECRET, AND TOOK HER TO ENGLAND—JUST LIKE THAT!

HOW ROMANTIC!

Panel 11:
HOW CRAZY!

CRAZY?—I'M CONVINCED, EL. ALL THE TRULY ROMANTIC MEN ARE OVER 80!

Panel 12:
THEY KNOW HOW TO DANCE, THEY BRING YOU FLOWERS, THEY NEVER SWEAR... IN THE OLD DAYS, MEN TREATED US LIKE "LADIES".

YES....

Panel 13:
BUT FEW OF THEM TREATED US LIKE EQUALS.

THE BEST THING ABOUT TRAVELLING AT MY AGE...IS LOOKING FORWARD TO GOING HOME!

ALL GATES →

INTERNATIONAL

CHECKING TWO BAGS PLEASE! WE WERE ON OUR HONEYMOON!
CONGRATULATIONS!

IRIS, DO YOU HAVE TO TELL EVERYONE?!!
I WON'T IF YOU DON'T WANT ME TO, JIM

MR. AND MRS. RICHARDS? THE AIRCRAFT IS FULL, SO WE'RE PUTTING YOU IN FIRST CLASS! (IT'S A WEDDING PRESENT!)
TORONTO 11:45 ON TIME FLT 832
GATE D23

LICORICE ALLSORTS, SIR?
YES-AND BY THE WAY WE WERE ON OUR HONEYMOON!
SWEET
J.BEANS ALLSORTS JUBE

WE PICKED UP GRAMPA AN' IRIS AT THE AIRPORT AN' TOOK THEM HOME!

HOW ARE THE HONEY-MOONERS? TIRED AND GROUCHY FROM TRAVELLING, BUT THEY'RE FINE.

THE WEIRD THING IS... WHEN THEY GOT TO THEIR BUILDING, THEY DECIDED TO GO TO THEIR OWN SEPARATE APART-MENTS!

WHAT KIND OF A MARRIAGE IS **THAT**?!!

A GOOD ONE, APRIL... AND IT'S GOING TO LAST A LONG, LONG TIME!

CHEESEBURGER, ROOT BEER AND FRIES, PLEASE.

UM, I'LL HAVE THE VEGGIE PLATTER WITH WATER, PLEASE.

MFF CRUNCH MUNCH

ARE YOU GONNA FINISH YOUR FRIES, RUDY?

NOPE! DIG IN!

TAKE A COUPLE OF NUGGETS, LIZ. I'M FULL!

WANT TO FINISH MY DESSERT?

UH.... SURE!

SIGH — I DON'T KNOW WHY I CAN'T LOSE WEIGHT....

PLEASE

ALL I EVER ORDER IS A SALAD!

WHISPER GIGGLE WHISPER GIGGLE GIGGLE WHISPER

WHISPER, WHISPER GIGGLE WHISPER!

HEY, GIRLS! HOW'S IT GOIN'?

OH, MAN—THAT WAS WEIRD! ONE OF THEM ACTUALLY SPOKE TO US!!!

I TOTALLY LIKE YOUR HAIRCUT, BECKY! SERIOUSLY?

IT LOOKS GREAT. ESPECIALLY SINCE IT'S BLONDE AN' NATURALLY CURLY! YEAH.

IT MAKES YOU LOOK....YOUNGER!

HUFF SNORT!!

MAN, AFTER A REMARK LIKE THAT, I THINK YOU SHOULD GO AN' APOLOGIZE!

I JUST PICKED UP APRIL AND HER FRIENDS FROM THE MALL. WHERE IS SHE?

SHE RAN UPSTAIRS TO BED. APPARENTLY THERE WAS A DISAGREEMENT, AND BY THE TIME I ARRIVED, THEY WEREN'T SPEAKING TO EACH OTHER.

IT'S NOT EASY BEING 11, IS IT. YOU'RE TOO YOUNG TO BE A WOMAN AND, TOO OLD TO BE A CHILD. YOU WANT EVERYONE TO LIKE YOU...BUT SOMETIMES, YOU FIND IT HARD TO LIKE YOURSELF!

...NOTHING HEALS LIKE A HUG!

WAIT! DON'T TOUCH IT!!!

MY GRANDMOTHER USED TO SAY, "IF A SPIDER FALLS IN FRONT OF YOU, IT'S AN IMPORTANT SIGN"

IF IT DROPS DOWN, YOU HAVE BAD LUCK.... IF IT GOES BACK UP, YOUR LUCK WILL BE GOOD

IT'S GONE BACK UP! THIS IS EXCELLENT—MEANS VERY GOOD LUCK, DEANNA!!—NOW YOU CAN SMACK IT!

ISN'T THAT BAD LUCK?

YES...BUT ONLY FOR THE SPIDER.

IS THIS YOUR FIRST TIME PRACTICE TEACHING?

YES... I'VE TUTORED BEFORE, BUT NEVER ACTUALLY TAUGHT A CLASS.

OUR LADY OF SORROWS IS A GREAT SCHOOL. THE STAFF WILL HELP YOU WITH LESSON PLANS AND GIVE YOU QUITE A BIT OF FREEDOM

IT'S NOT YOUR TYPICAL SCHOOL. IT'S A CULTURAL MIX OF ENGLISH, FRENCH AND OJIBWAY.

I THINK, FOR THE FIRST DAY, YOU'LL JUST BE AN OBSERVER.

...AND, BE OBSERVED

HI, GRETA! I SEE YOU'VE BROUGHT US OUR NEW STUDENT TEACHER! ELIZABETH, I'M NANCY. LET ME INTRODUCE YOU TO SOME OF OUR STAFF.

BOOZHOO!

BIENVENUE!

WELCOME!

HELLO

good book is a good

LET ME TAKE YOU ON A TOUR, AND AFTER LUNCH, YOU'LL GO TO YOUR FIRST CLASS.

THANKS GRETA. WHAT A LOVELY SCHOOL!

—AND THE CHILDREN ARE ADORABLE!

WAIT 'TIL YOU FACE THEM IN LARGE GROUPS!

THIS IS OUR NATIVE STUDIES AREA. THE KIDS LEARN ABOUT THEIR CULTURE, CUSTOMS, LANGUAGE AND THINGS LIKE THAT.

THERE WERE ONCE SEVERAL HUNDRED FIRST NATIONS LANGUAGES IN NORTH AMERICA, BUT ONLY A FEW SURVIVED.

WHY?

ONE REASON IS THAT THERE WAS NO WRITTEN TEXT, NO PHYSICAL RECORD—EVERYTHING WAS PASSED ON BY WORD OF MOUTH.

SHHHHH!!!

CLASS, THIS IS MISS PATTERSON. SHE'S GOING TO BE VISITING WITH US!

HELLO, EVERY-ONE!

MY NAME IS ELIZABETH AND I'M STUDYING TO BE A TEACHER. I'M GOING TO BE PRACTICE TEACHING HERE AT YOUR SCHOOL.

MY HOBBIES ARE SINGING, SKATING, SKIING, SWIMMING—AND, I REALLY LIKE TO READ. —DOES ANYONE HAVE ANY QUESTIONS THEY'D LIKE TO ASK ME?

YEAH... DO YOU HAVE A BOYFRIEND?!

WELCOME TO TEACHING!

ARE YOU GOING TO BE TEACHING US TODAY?

NO. TODAY I'M JUST WATCHING

WILL YOU BE TEACHING US TOMORROW?

I'LL BE DOING MATH WITH YOU TOMORROW.

ECHO, PLEASE EXPLAIN 100% AND 50%

100% IS... LIKE THE WHOLE THING, AN' 50% IS LIKE...HALF.

EXCELLENT. THAT'S VERY GOOD.

NOW, I'D LIKE 100% OF YOUR ATTENTION UP HERE, PLEASE.

GULP!

I HOPE YOU ENJOYED YOUR OBSERVATION DAY, ELIZABETH!

I DID, THANK YOU. I'M REALLY LOOKING FORWARD TO WORKING WITH YOU!

TOMORROW, WE HAVE YOU DOING GRADE ONE READING, GRADE THREE MATH...AND WE THOUGHT YOU COULD DO SOME PLAYGROUND DUTY!

OK, I HAVE LESSON PLANS FOR BOTH CLASSES... WHAT DO YOU THINK IS GOING TO BE THE BIGGEST CHALLENGE?!

I'D SAY PLAYGROUND.

DEFINITELY.

GOOD LUCK.

Panel 1: I'M GLAD YOU DON'T MIND DRIVING ME TO THE SCHOOL WITH YOU, GRETA.

NO PROBLEM. I'M GOING THERE ANYWAY! —AND, I LIKE THE COMPANY.

Panel 2: SEEMS STRANGE TO BE COMMUTING EVERY DAY TO THE TOWN I GREW UP IN. BUT, I MARRIED A GUY WHO WORKS IN NORTH BAY, SO....

Panel 3: I GREW UP IN GARDEN VILLAGE, JUST OUTSIDE STURGEON FALLS. IT'S A PRETTY PLACE. I COULD TAKE YOU THERE SOMETIME.

I'D LIKE THAT.

Panel 4: WHAT BRINGS YOU ALL THE WAY UP HERE, ELIZABETH?

....THIS.

Panel 5: HOW WAS YOUR FIRST DAY ON THE JOB, LIZ?

OK... I FELT PRETTY WEIRD BECAUSE I WAS JUST AN OBSERVER

Panel 6: TOMORROW, I ACTUALLY GET TO TEACH. I'LL BE WINGIN' IT SOLO.

HOO...20 PAIRS OF EYEBALLS STARING AT YOU!

Panel 7: TO BE HONEST, I'M SCARED, CANDACE. WHAT IF THE KIDS THINK I'M A TOTAL IDIOT?!

THEN, KUDOS, BABY!

Panel 8: WITH WHAT THEY SEE ON TELEVISION... THAT'S THE ONLY WAY TO GRAB THEIR ATTENTION.

Panel 9: THE WAY I SEE IT, A TEACHER HAS TO BE AN ENTERTAINER. YOU GOTTA HAVE EXPRESSION, BE EXCITED ABOUT YOUR SUBJECT— I MEAN, IF YOU SOUND BORED, THEY'LL BE BORED, SAVVY?

Panel 10: MOVE AROUND THE ROOM! EXPLAIN STUFF CLEARLY, IMAGINATIVELY, AN' WITH A SENSE OF HUMOR!

Panel 11: I LOVE THE GUYS WHO ARE KEEN AN' EXPRESSIVE, MAN, LIKE– I STAY AWAKE, I GET PUMPED! I GET INTO IT, AN' I REALLY WANNA **LEARN!**

YEAH

Panel 12: I HAD A PROF LIKE THAT, ONCE.

131

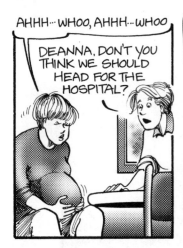

AHHH…WHOO, AHHH…WHOO

DEANNA, DON'T YOU THINK WE SHOULD HEAD FOR THE HOSPITAL?

THE CONTRACTIONS ARE ABOUT 30 MINUTES APART, MICHAEL. I THINK WE HAVE SOME TIME.

I'M PACKING THE CAR. I WANT TO BE THERE AND READY.

MICHAEL, CALM DOWN! YOU'RE IN SUCH A PANIC!

I KNOW. I CAN'T HELP IT.

—I'VE NEVER HAD A BABY BEFORE!!!

HELLO, DEANNA! WE HAVE A ROOM ALL READY FOR YOU!

FAIRLAWN GENERAL HOSPITAL.   BYRNE STREET ENTRANCE.

HAVE YOU CONTACTED YOUR FAMILY?

NOT YET. WE WANTED THIS TO BE A…

BREATHE, HONEY, BREATHE!

OK, WE'RE ON OUR WAY TO DELIVERY! WANNA SAY ANYTHING, HONEY?

AAAUGH!

WAIT—LET'S GET YOU ON SPEAKER PHONE!

…PRIVATE EXPERIENCE.

LOOK AT THE CAMERA, BABE. CAN YOU MANAGE A WAVE?

YOU'RE DOING WELL, DEANNA, WE'RE ALMOST THERE!

PUSH HARD WHEN I TELL YOU TO, OK?

OWWHHH…I NEVER KNEW THIS WOULD HURT SO MUCH!

WHAT CAN I DO?—RUB YOUR BACK?

HOLD MY HAND, MICHAEL!

OK!

OWOOOOHHHH

DON'T WORRY…THAT WAS ME!

WELCOME "HOME", BABY!

WELL, WE'RE A MOTHER AND FATHER, NOW. OUR LIVES WILL BE CHANGING

HIC! ERK! AH-WAAH AH-WAAH AH-WAAH AH-WAH!

AH-WAAAA, AH-WAAA

AND CHANGING AND CHANGING AND CHANGING!